Small-Scale Silversmithing

Small-Scale Silversmithing

FJ Whitelaw

THE CROWOOD PRESS

First published in 2019 by
The Crowood Press Ltd
Ramsbury, Marlborough
Wiltshire SN8 2HR

enquiries@crowood.com

www.crowood.com

This impression 2022

British Library Cataloguing-in-Publication Data
A catalogue record for this book is available from the British Library.

ISBN 978 1 78500 617 3

Graphic design and typesetting by Peggy & Co. Design Inc.
Printed and bound in India by Parksons Graphics Pvt. Ltd.

Contents

Introduction

Silversmithing is the practice of creating objects in silver other than jewellery. Traditional silversmithing has evolved over a long period of time but at its core, it is the manipulation of metal to create objects of use, importance and beauty.

The history of precious metal artefacts includes many types of objects from the most grandiose trophies and ecclesiastical treasures to the smallest snuffbox or salt spoon. Many surviving examples of historical pieces are not just large statements of wealth and status but are more personal, portable treasures. These small items do not hold a place of lesser significance in the history of silverwares but are objects intended for the domestic setting, both for use and to announce the excellent taste of the fortunate owner. There is also a particular category of small silversmithing referred to as 'objects of virtue' which are small but perfectly formed examples of exquisite craftsmanship, made using the combined skills of the silversmith, engraver, enameller and many others. The focus of this book is on learning about the techniques employed by the silversmith to make a selection of smaller items that may not demand so much specialist equipment or machinery.

Metalworking in all its forms has evolved from early experiments which are now lost to time. Little is known about the mysterious origins of finding and using metal, in part because one of the unique properties of this family of elements is that metal can be melted down and reused again and again.

The discovery of metal in its basic state of ore from rock, or in a seam deep in a mountain, is in itself remarkable. That this unpromising raw material was then transformed into a usable plastic material remains one of the great discoveries of humankind. Producing metal from mere rock signalled huge changes to the cultural and technical development of human society, taking us from the Neolithic period into a new era of finding, mining and refining. Metal quickly became a sought-after commodity across many different cultures, creating the need for trade across seas and continents.

Metal can be reused and recycled as many times as needed, provided that there is a reliable heat source. It is likely that gold was the first metal to be discovered and worked, probably around 8,000 years ago although this is impossible to prove with any certainty. It has the advantage of being present in rivers and alluvial deposits so can be found in its pure state without being mined or refined. Gold has the advantage of a distinctive colour making it easily visible in the landscape, unlike many other metals that hide within parent rock, or are deep below the surface. Early experiments will have revealed the transformative power of both heat and stone hammers on this exotic new material, which can be formed and reformed as desired.

Copper was probably the next metal to be isolated. It is a little harder than gold and being found in greater abundance made it perfect for the creation of tools, implements, catches and adornments. This diversity of application is where the journey of metalworking makes its first strides. The discovery and use of silver followed not long afterwards, probably around 4,000 BC, followed by the development of bronze, an alloy of copper and tin. Bronze overshadowed silver because it is suitable for more durable tools, mechanisms and of course valuable weapons. Metalworking became widespread across the world as societies were able to support the time, ingenuity and skill needed to produce these objects. Those skills learned by trial and error over generations would have been applied to the newly discovered silver. It was not universally available and its softness in its pure state meant that its value developed as the skill of working and alloying it grew. The evidence of silver's increasing popularity over time is the emergence of its use as currency, as well as being a medium for fashioning treasured items.

Artefacts made from silver signify a civilization that supports and values knowledge and artistry. Archaeology has revealed that silver objects were highly valued in many ways and used as grave goods to bestow their owners with status in the afterlife. The flexible, forgiving nature of silver means that as a medium to craft, it is soft enough to work from flat sheet into complex three-dimensional forms and it will retain that shape indefinitely. Silversmithing has evolved due to its most appealing feature of being particularly malleable and reasonably easy to alloy with small amounts of copper to subtly adjust its plasticity. Silver can be fairly thin and yet is strong enough to retain its form and withstand use day after day. In addition to its working properties, its colour – or rather lack of it – has contributed to its allure. Subtler than its more sumptuous partner gold, silver reminds us of the moon, water and the ethereal, leading silver to become associated with notions of purity, magic and religious potency. The clarity of silver's whiteness renders it almost without colour when polished as the world around it is reflected back untainted by any hue. In recent times, some of this belief has been scientifically corroborated and silver is used for its purifying and antibacterial properties in medicine and technology.

Over centuries, silversmiths have developed the skills that are still relevant today. The arrival of the Industrial Revolution could have diminished the value and role of the smith as a skilled craftsperson but even in the age of mass-produced goods, the power and beauty of handmade objects still holds true. Indeed a renewed interest in contemporary design and respect for uniquely crafted objects has helped to bring silversmithing to a new and wider audience. Many contemporary silversmiths still use these same techniques in their practice whilst augmenting them with the latest technology. This has opened the door into a twenty-first century renaissance of design and technology working harmoniously together.

Working with metal to create objects totally from scratch is deeply satisfying for the beginner and expert alike. In this book, the emphasis is on starting small to allow time to build up understanding and skill without the pressure of the material costs or expensive equipment. Each chapter introduces a technique and explains how it can be used and what can be realistically achieved through a series of simply laid out projects.

Throughout the book the words 'silver' and 'metal' are used pretty much interchangeably. In the majority of cases, either silver, copper or gilding metal can be used for projects with equally good results. Silver costs far more than copper or gilding metal but these metals all share very similar properties and are all suitable for silversmithing projects. Before starting, it is worth taking time to consider what will be needed to create small-scale silversmithing in your own workshop.

CHAPTER 1

Getting Started

This book contains numerous illustrations, many of which are very simplified diagrams. There are photographs of tools in this introductory chapter and thereafter are mostly shown in either a sketch or diagram. Not all of the diagrams are exactly to scale where this is not necessary. The main function of the illustrations is to show the silver and how it is positioned in relation to the tools or equipment being used to form it. None of the illustrations show hands, as the focus tends to be on the process or object. Hammers are held at the end of the handle, not near the hammer head, therefore no fingers need to be visible. Of course, metal being worked is frequently held in place by hand and this will be explained in the accompanying text where relevant. The diagrams for setting pieces up to solder have been shown as possible examples of how to position work on the hearth but the magical moment that solder melts is hard to capture in a static image, so again this is described rather than illustrated. The projects introduce techniques starting at the beginning with first experiments in creating three-dimensional forms from flat sheet and building towards objects constructed from several forming methods.

SETTING UP A WORKSHOP

Working with silver or copper will require a dedicated place to work. This room or space need not be large but should be dry, well ventilated and ideally with natural light. Sometimes it will be noisy. This is not really a problem for the practitioner, because one's own noise is less noticeable and there are ear defenders to protect against the sound of hammering. It is how near the workshop will be to those who may not share an enthusiasm for hours of sustained hammering, which might mean some form of sound insulation is needed. Once a suitable place for the workshop has been found, try to arrange the space with four or more distinct workshop areas that will be for the following activities:

- A workbench for standing work such as hammering, filing and working at a vice.
- A seated work place with a bench peg for precision work such as measuring, cutting, filing and fitting.
- The hearth for hot work such as heating hardened metal to soften it and soldering to join parts together. The hearth should have water adjacent; either a sink or large bowl will do.
- There should be space that can be used for cleaning and polishing; this is the dirtiest work and must not be next to any soldering or hot work.

In addition to these areas there will need to be a clean area for design, drawing or model making – this could be a simple board that can be stowed away when not in use.

The workbench and seated work place

The workbench must be a solid bench fitted with an engineer's vice. This is used to hold either tools or the piece of work, so that objects can be gripped securely. This is where some of the making and hammering will take place. A woodworking bench is probably too low so is generally regarded as not suitable, but could be adapted or raised up for metalworking. The bench will need space for specific tools such as a flat plate for flattening, sanding or any measuring that has to be done on an absolutely flat surface. The workbench can also incorporate a 'cutout' in the style of a jeweller's workbench for sawing, filing and small precision hand working. A typical jeweller's bench has a semi-circular cutout with a bench peg to support sawing and filing, a bench 'apron' or 'leather' to collect offcuts and a low seat for a comfortable working posture.

The 'cutout' is an area for working when seated whereas working at the vice is usually done standing up, although if that is a problem it can be arranged so that the equipment is organized to be at the correct height for seated working. If space is limited, many smaller hand tools can be kept safely off the workbench on shelves, racks, wall magnets or suspended at the bench cutout. Heavier items should be kept handy enough to be within reach to avoid too much lifting and carrying, but not in the way of any activity. For sensible health and safety practice it is a good idea to keep weighty items near to the point of use to avoid unnecessary heavy lifting. Hammers, mallets, stakes and steel-forming tools must be kept dry and accessible so that surfaces and hammer faces cannot get damaged. It is fairly easy to make a rack for hammers and mallets so that they are ready to use yet out of the way, keeping the bench top free of clutter. An under-bench trolley is ideal for storing less frequently used tools or bulky items. Adding stout casters to an old recycled cupboard or low table is another storage solution when space is at a premium. Generally speaking, many activities may be done standing at the workbench using the engineer's vice or using a steel flat plate, so opt for a bench height that is comfortable for working without stooping. The main workbench and the jeweller's cutout are the two areas where much of the making will be done.

The workbench.

The hearth

This is an area for heating metal and must be covered with a fireproof surface such as firebricks or non-asbestos boards. There are commercially produced hearths that include a gas torch, and may also have an extractor fan and turntable. The cost of a new ready-made hearth at a couple of thousand pounds may not be appropriate for the first-time smith, especially if the budget is restricted. If a second-hand one is not readily available then it is fairly straightforward to make a sturdy hearth area from a single unit of a heavy-duty shelving system. The uprights consist of a steel frame that is held in place with horizontal steel shelf supports. The shelving is usually woodchip, which can be painted with a fire-retardant layer before completely covering with sheets of a non-asbestos fireproof material. Fire bricks and sheets of fireproof material for chimneys or garden ovens can be bought from DIY stores and builders' yards. Build up an insulated wall at the back of the hearth and half of each side to create a lined alcove for doing all the heating. The hollow area can then be adapted for each project by having a selection of soldering blocks to build up a platform to support the work, regardless of shape or size.

The hearth should always have a sink, bowl or tank of water immediately next to it for cooling hot metal and there should also be an easily reachable place for tongs, tweezers and any other equipment relating to hot work. Ideally the hearth should not be too bright, so do not site this part of your workshop right under a bright light unless it can be switched off. If it is convenient to be next to a window that provides ventilation, fit a blind so that the area can be dimmed when necessary. Working in poor light is generally a bad idea, but in this instance it is a great help because when heating a metal object it is vital to judge the correct temperature and this is easier to do if the surrounding area is fairly dark. The hearth does not need to be permanently gloomy – just when it is in use – so the area can have good light for setting work up that can be switched on and off as needed.

The heating area must have some form of ventilation, at the most basic a window to open, but a better solution is to install a domestic cooker hood if the hearth does not have inbuilt extraction.

As mentioned earlier a ready-made braising hearth will likely be supplied with a torch to attach to the fuel, usually gas and oxygen. It is still possible to achieve high enough temperatures with propane on its own as long as the torch nozzle is large enough. This is probably the easiest option to begin with if building a hearth from scratch and means only investing in a bottle of propane and a torch kit with a selection of nozzles to suit different scales of project. Gas bottles can be put away after use if they are to be stored elsewhere overnight. A wheeled trolley is ideal for moving the gas bottle if it is too heavy to lift comfortably.

1. The heat source should be easy to turn on and off.
2. Keep water nearby to 'quench' hot work and in case of fire.
3 Make sure there is some ventilation.
3. Check that the area is childproof if necessary.
4. Keep a first-aid box nearby.

A hearth lined with fire bricks with a turntable.

Polishing and finishing

Some silversmiths will send their finished pieces to a professional polisher because it is a highly skilled area of work. Of course, not all smiths will do this but prefer to complete pieces in house. A polishing motor is an incredibly useful tool for creating very shiny surfaces, but it can also be a dangerous piece of equipment that should not be used without proper training. A polishing machine has a central motor that turns two projecting spindles at either side. There are a range of 'mops' which can be fitted onto the spindles when the motor is switched off. Some mops are slightly abrasive or 'cutting' and will remove more metal from the surface of an object or act like a fine emery paper. These mops can speed up the finishing process immensely because firestain is removed quickly and efficiently. Other mops are for general buffing and used with a product such as 'Tripoli' which is for harder felt mops to provide a first polish. The final step in polishing is done with a soft mop, sometimes called 'swansdown' and used with a very fine polish such as rouge to leave the finished piece with a very high shine.

A polishing motor needs space around it to work safely, with an electric socket nearby so there are no trailing cables. It must be bolted onto a bench or mounted on a solid stand so that it remains steady at all times while in use. Polishing is a process that can be dirty and create a large amount of dust, so it is important to wear a dust mask and safety goggles when in use and be able to clean the area thoroughly afterwards. Most polishers large enough for silversmithing will have a built-in extraction unit but second-hand ones may not. An extractor fan or cheap vacuum cleaner can be set up to remove dust while it is in operation or it may be possible to mount the polishing motor on a movable bench which can be taken outside for working. Health and safety practice is paramount with all motor-driven equipment so as well as protective goggles and dust mask, keep hair, scarves and garments well away from the rotating wheel. It is also worth repeating that a dedicated training course on how to use a polishing motor safely and effectively is highly recommended. A lovingly wrought piece of work can be quickly ruined by a high-speed buff in the hands of an inexperienced polisher.

The alternative to motorized polishing is to do it by hand. For smaller items this is not so difficult and although it is of course slower, the results will be just as pleasing. In many cases a highly buffed surface may not be the desired end result so those hammered finishes will need little further attention. The final chapter deals with hand polishing in more detail.

The tree trunk

Traditionally, smiths' workshops will have a tree trunk to use as a support for an anvil or various stakes or tools. The top surface of the tree trunk can be customized with hollow forms or grooves carved out for different forming activities to help shape sheet metal. Sometimes a stake is permanently fixed into the tree trunk and if there is space, it is a good place to work on a steel flat plate. The reason why the tree trunk has been a part of the smith's workshop since ancient times is that the solid wood will absorb noise and vibration from hammering. Any tree trunk will do as long as it is high enough to sit at, and has a reasonable surface area of at least the size of a large dinner plate. A newly felled chunk of tree must have both ends cut flat so that it will stand upright and be stable. Remove all the bark before setting it aside to fully dry out over several months or seasons. If it is resting outside make sure it is raised above the ground to allow the air to get around it and keep it protected from rain, so that it does not start to rot.

If a tree trunk is not a viable option due to space or availability, then working at the main workbench is perfectly acceptable. To limit the noise from hammering the workbench can stand on rubber matting or an old carpet. This is not quite as effective as having a tree trunk but a good alternative, especially if there is more than one vice on the bench.

A tree trunk absorbs sound and vibration.

The rolling mill

A rolling mill may not be absolutely essential, but it is a desirable piece of equipment for any workshop. It is used to reduce the gauge of sheet, wire or rod and will last a lifetime. The rolling mill can be used for decorative work by embossing textures onto sheet as well as thinning it. Since it is a heavy piece of machinery it must either be mounted on a solid-metal stand or on a very sturdy bench. Rust and dust can damage the rollers which are engineered to give a flawless finish so protect it when not in use, keep it oiled, covered and in a dry environment. Mills are expensive when new but it is possible to find second-hand ones for sale. There is also the resale value and any purchase that has been well maintained can be sold on when no longer required.

The rolling mill is for reducing silver sheet or wire.

The anvil

This is the very symbol of metalworking and the heaviest single piece of solid metal equipment. It can be sat on a tree trunk of its own or mounted on a bench. An anvil is not always a realistic option for every workshop and there are alternatives for providing a good support for hammering different forms. Having a selection of stakes that can be used in the vice or fitted into a tree trunk can take the place of an anvil and provide more or less the same function. A new anvil will have a reasonably sized flat area and a conical projection at the other end. Old anvils can have damaged or rough surfaces so will only be suitable for preliminary working but if a second-hand anvil is available, make sure there is a way it can be transported safely as sellers usually do not want to include delivery for obvious reasons. As with all steel tools it is a good idea to look after the surface and keep it free from moisture, which will cause rust and pitting. Wipe over the surface with an oily rag when it is not in regular use.

Electric drill

An electric drill or pedestal drill is mounted onto its own solid stand or a solid bench so it is permanently fixed in a stable situation for safety. A good bench drill will provide accurate vibration-free drilling for all sizes of work and with a changeable chuck can accommodate most sizes of drill bit. Bench drills are used for light engineering, model making and wood working, so this item does not need to come from a specialist silversmithing supplier although the drill bits should always be specifically for metal.

A small bench drill is ideal if space is limited.

Hand tools

Hand tools will make up the majority of equipment for the smith, as this covers almost everything apart from the bigger fixtures and fittings mentioned above.

Before making anything in the workshop it will be necessary to measure, mark and cut the material. Many of these basic items can come from the local hardware store, such as the following toolbox essentials:

Steel ruler. 12in or 30cm long steel ruler will help with precision; a plastic one will not be as durable and can get damaged easily.

Compass and dividers. These are used for drawing circles and arcs. Dividers are adjustable with two sharp points for scribing circles rather than a compass, which has one point and a pencil holder. The dividers are also useful for taking exact measurements.

Engineer's scribe. The scribe or scriber is a sharp-pointed steel tool for marking fine lines on metal. One end goes to a straight point and the other point is set at 90 degrees.

Engineer's square. This is another tool for accurate measuring and in this case it helps to ascertain right angles. Some may incorporate a spirit level, which is also very useful. The base edge of a 'square' is usually thicker so that it can be balanced on the edge of a bench while the metal being marked can be held in place securely. It can be used standing on the heavy base.

All of the above tools are widely available and as the names suggest, are used in engineering and precision work.

After measuring and marking, metal must be cut to size.

Shears and tinsnips

Shears are for cutting pieces of sheet metal, with tinsnips being for smaller work. These are only for cutting out roughly and are not routinely used to cut intricate shapes or exact straight edges because of the distortion that can occur. Some workshops have a guillotine mounted on the bench, which is very useful for cutting longer straight edges, but this is not

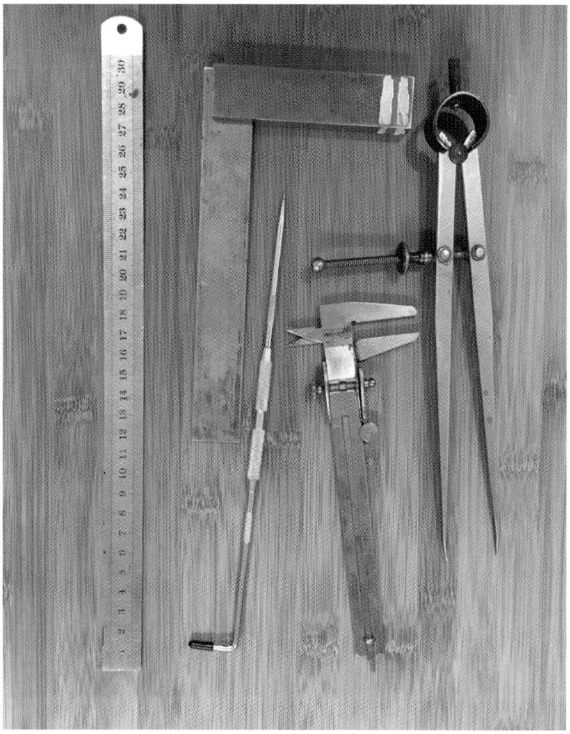

Measuring and marking equipment.

Piercing saws with a chenier vice and tinsnips.

essential because bullion dealers will sell silver cut to the dimensions requested.

Piercing saw

This is probably one of the handiest tools for cutting out sheet. With practice it can be used for straight edges and intricate decorative work too. Large silversmithing workshops will probably have a free-standing electric saw for cutting large pieces of sheet but the humble hand-held piercing saw can do almost all jobs including finely detailed shapes and patterns. There are extra-deep saw frames for tackling larger pieces of metal. For the beginner, this is one tool that it is worth practicing with. Once mastered it can be used with speed and efficiency, opening up all sort of possibilities for design and construction. There are different sizes of blade for the piercing saw but the medium grade of 0/3 is a good size to start with.

Hand files

Once a piece of copper or silver has been cut out, the edges will need to be refined and smoothed with a file. Every tool kit should contain a selection of good-quality files of different sizes and degrees of coarseness. It is also important to have files of different shapes such as a flat or pillar file, half round and safety back which only has cutting teeth on one surface.

There are plenty of cheap files on the market but buying a few good-quality files is worth it, as they will be made from hardened steel and if cared for properly will last for years. There are longer files of 250mm/10in, 200mm/8in and 150mm/6in, which between them are suitable for most jobs. The length includes the 'tang' or end, which is inserted into a wooden handle. A coarse file is known as a 'bastard' or '0' cut and a second cut is of medium coarseness. The smooth or '4' cut file is the least rough and will remove less metal and leave fewer marks on the surface. Always hold the file in one hand with the other hand supporting the tip when filing work held in the vice. This will keep the file level and avoid any uncontrolled action, which can damage an edge or remove too much material. All filing is done by pushing the file away in a sweeping motion. This is because the tiny teeth have a direction for cutting, so pushing away will remove particles of metal and the return action will do nothing. Metal being filed may be held in a vice or held steady by hand at the bench while it is being worked. To care for a file and remove the tiny fragments of metal captured in the teeth, it can be cleaned with a file brush. This is a flat brush with short wire bristles that cleans away filings and stops the file teeth from becoming clogged up with debris.

A selection of files of different shapes and sizes.

Needle files

Needle files are small jewellers' files that come in a wider variety of cross sections and can be used for small spaces that need to be precision worked. Needle files are often sold in packs of six or twelve different shapes for detailed and precise work where something larger would not be suitable. Swiss files are usually the best quality and most expensive but there are cheaper versions from specialist suppliers or general tool shops. The cheaper versions are likely to be fairly coarse whereas the dearer ones will be available in different cuts for fine work. A 'riffler' file is a specialist curved file and can be useful for smaller work, but is not absolutely essential. Good quality riffler files are quite expensive and may not be used much. They come with different curved ends to reach almost any imaginable nook or cranny.

Abrasives

After filing a piece of metal there will be some tiny grooves or tool marks left on the surface so there are a variety of ways to remove these before the final polish. There are scratchy 'Scotch scrubber' wheels for polishing motors, sanding belts or 'linishers' that will do a similar job by machine. At some stage there will have to be some hand finishing with one or more type of different abrasive. Emery paper or wet and dry paper comes in a range of different grits. The coarsest have a lower number on the back such as 100 or 240, with medium grades from 400, 600 or 800. The smoother grades start at 1,000 and run up to emery papers as smooth as 5,000 or 7,000. To emery a surface is slower than using a machine but it can be done efficiently by making polishing sticks from 30cm lengths of flat dowel covered in different grades of emery paper. The coarseness, from 240 grit which is fairly rough through to 2,000 grit which is fairly smooth, will provide a good range of grades. After using a file the emery paper could start at around 400 grit up to at least 3,000 grit.

The finish of fine emery paper may provide the desired final surface of a piece or be used before a final polish with a soft cloth. During construction of an object it is frequently necessary to emery edges absolutely flat. A larger emery board can be made by sticking a full-sized piece of rough 100 grit emery permanently to a flat piece of plastic or wooden board. This is a quick way to guarantee a levelled edge and is easy to make from one or more grades of abrasive. A decorative finish can be achieved with a rubber grit block, which is easier to hold and comes in different degrees of coarseness.

Punch tools

These are used with a hammer or mallet to make depressions in the surface of metal. It may just be a centre punch to mark where a hole will be drilled, which is important when an accurate marker is needed. They are also used decoratively and can be purchased or made from rods ground into shape at the end and finished to a high polish. Heavy-duty nails or other pieces of steel can be customized for punching textures and patterns into the surface of an almost-finished object.

A selection of punches for decoration and forming metal.

Gravers and scorpers

Engraving tools or 'scorpers' are small hand-held tools. They are sharp enough to scoop out a tiny scraping of metal from a surface. Gravers are pushed into the surface at an angle to create a small groove in the metal. There are many different shapes of these tools, with the cutting end sharpened so that a specific shape or angle of groove can be created such as a 'v' shape or 'u' shape. Engraving is a specialist skill that can take years to perfect and although some smiths use this to great effect, it is not practised universally due to the time needed to become proficient. However, these are not expensive tools so it need not break the bank to buy a couple of different shapes and start experimenting. There is a dedicated organization that can advise on courses and a wealth of instructional videos online to learn more.

Mallets

Hammers are at the heart of almost all silversmithing and although it is possible to use basic household hammers for some elementary things, such as some rudimentary flattening, for most occasions only a specialist one will do. Firstly, the difference between a hammer and a mallet is that hammers are made from steel and mallets from a soft material such as wood, horn, rawhide, plastic or rubber. Mallets come in different weights and sizes with different functions. A mallet is used to form material without marking the surface or making much difference to its dimensions. There are some exceptions to this, but for a starter silversmith the workshop should have a small selection for different functions such as a small to medium rawhide mallet for wire and thinner sheet, a round-ended wooden mallet for first forming of hollow or concave forms and something heavier such as a weighted 'dead blow' rubber mallet where more pressure is needed.

A selection of mallets.

Hammers

There are hundreds of specialist hammers to choose from. Avoid being bamboozled by this huge diversity and focus on a few to cover the basic range of activities. It is also important not be tempted to buy a really heavy hammer unless it is comfortable to use repeatedly; the weight will become more apparent with each strike which will lead to inaccuracy. Traditionally, hammers have wooden handles because the wood will absorb some of the shock from each hammer blow. This is important for avoiding strains and injury. Wood can also be customized if necessary so that the grip is perfect. The handle of the hammer is known as the shaft and the striking surface of the hammer head is the face or pein (pronounced *peen*).

Of the basic workshop hammers, a heavy–medium weight ball pein hammer will be useful for lots of general forming and flattening. This type of hammer has one round flat face and one that is domed/ball pein. A lightweight version of the same hammer is a handy tool for lighter tapping jobs and some texturing. General tool or DIY stores probably stock these and lightweight 'cross pein hammers', which are also useful for texturing. Hammers from a hardware store may cost less but are likely to need smoothing on different grades of emery paper before use on silver. This is because each time the metal is struck, it will be impressed by the hammer surface. All hammers need some care and occasional refacing to keep them fit for use and with a grinding wheel, they can be customized further if desired.

The essential hammers (which cannot be sourced from a hardware store) are the 'raising' hammer and the 'planishing' hammer. A raising hammer is the heavier at around 500 grammes and has two long, narrow horizontal peins. The raising face is flatter than the other side, which can be used for forming, forging and stretching metal. This forging surface is like a large version of a cross pein hammer and is generally used to thin and work metal in wire or rod form. Although a raising hammer will come ready-shaped for use in the workshop, it may have slightly sharper edges and corners than is ideal for a beginner. Any misplaced blow could leave an unwanted line or blemish in the silver so check that edges are rounded off and there is a shiny, smooth finish before use. There are a huge number of hammers on the market, some of which come already prepared to a very high standard of finish but can cost twice as much as the more basic models. The main thing is to get specialist hammers from reputable suppliers of silversmithing tools, because they should be made from good-quality steel.

The planishing hammer usually weighs less than the raising hammer and is for finishing work after it has been made. Both faces are almost flat and medium sized, with one round face and the other square. This hammer is used to create a smooth surface after the main forming has been completed. By working with lots of light, overlapping hammer blows, a smooth surface is created in readiness for polishing. Planishing will flatten out slight irregularities and the process can be repeated until the desired effect is revealed, which is why it does not need to be very heavy.

The 'blocking' hammer has one or two ball pein ends and is for round forms or basic hollowing of sheet metal and sometimes has a longer head to reach into hollow forms. It is possible to use the basic workshop hammer for blocking holloware or the round-ended wooden mallet. A blocking hammer may not appear to be an absolute essential if the same function can be achieved by other ones, but is worth having as it will provide a different size of round end.

The 'repousse' hammer is used for chasing and repousse work. It has an extra-large flat face with a very small ball pein on the other side. The pronounced flat, round face is for striking the punches and the round-ended handle provides a balanced grip, allowing

A selection of hammers for a variety of functions.

comfortable tapping for hours at a time. The repousse hammer is only worth seeking out if this technique is going to be practised as it does not really have any other advantages.

Any good-quality hammers will feel well balanced with a wooden handle for some spring and a tightly fitting head. Second-hand hammers will be cheaper but with a little investment of time for cleaning and polishing the head and possibly making sure it is stable, they will give many years of service. Looking for second-hand tools also makes it easier to build up a more diverse collection of items like hammers.

Stakes

Stakes are the steel forms used to work on for various activities, from creating large vessels to small spoons. There are a huge number of stakes for all shapes and sizes of work and as these are expensive when new, it is worth looking out for any second-hand stakes. The easiest way to use them is in the bench vice for working when standing at the workbench. Of the small forming stakes, there are a few which are universal such as a 'mushroom' stake which, as its name suggests, is a hemisphere of steel supported on a square stalk for holding in the vice. There are other domed stakes, some of which will have a much longer handle that has the

Small stakes.

The engineer's vice

This has already been mentioned but this type of vice will be used a lot and it should be reasonably large and sturdy. A woodworking vice is not suitable for metalworking although may be handy for other activities. A 'leg vice' is a very tall, standing vice which can be attached to a bench or even a tree trunk, and will provide a very sturdy grip on tools which get a lot of hammering. Sometimes car boot sales are a good place to pick up second-hand tools.

added advantage of being useful for tall vessels. There are oval and rounded, and square shapes; stakes for spoons and convex or concave forms.

Then there are the larger 'raising' stakes which are specifically for transforming flat sheet into three-dimensional hollow vessels. These are often three-arm stakes or 'T' shaped, with a couple of different profiles for working on different sizes or shapes of object. In some instances stakes can be improvised or made from other materials but if they are for use with a metal hammer rather than a soft mallet, then they should be steel. Like the hammers, a stake should be kept smooth so that no blemishes are transferred to the silver. Stakes should be kept apart so that the working surfaces can't jostle against each other and get damaged, and like all steel equipment must be kept dry and rust free.

The flat plate

Even if there is an anvil in the workshop, then there should also be a steel flat plate. This will be used for flattening and forming but also for checking measurements from a reliable base as the work progresses. When buying a flat plate remember that silversmithing will require a larger size than a jeweller would use, so do not be tempted to get something too small.

Cleaning metal; the pickle tank

Heated metal becomes dull; this loss of surface shine and colour is called oxidation and is normally cleaned off in a solution of dilute sulphuric acid. This sulphuric acid is mixed in a ratio of twelve parts water to one part acid. The commonly used name for diluted sulphuric acid is 'pickle' and it is usually used warm because this cleans oxides or flux from the metal's surface more quickly. Many suppliers sell 'safety pickle', which is acid in crystal form. It is easier and safer to send by post and store dry until needed. The safety pickle crystal powder is diluted with water according to the manufacturer's guidelines to make up the pickle solution.

Some smiths may choose not to use sulphuric acid or safety pickle but instead use citric acid, which works a little slower but is more widely available in home brew shops or for other culinary purposes. Dedicated pickle tanks with a heat source and thermostat are available from tool suppliers but are expensive, so many smiths will use a ceramic or glass slow cooker to clean small to medium items of metalwork. For pickling large pieces of work some improvisation will be needed to construct something to accommodate large or awkwardly shaped items. A plastic storage box heated from below with a soil-warming unit for plant propagation may provide enough warmth for the pickle to do its job. Diluted pickle can be stored in the switched-off slow cooker or lidded container when not in use.

A large slow cooker can be used as a pickle tank.

Metal which has been cleaned in pickle must be rinsed free of acid, so always have a bowl of water nearby unless there is a sink where work can be rinsed. The only metal that goes into the pickle bath should be the object being cleaned – this means there should be no steel tongs or tweezers near the acid. Ferrous metals, such as steel and iron, will contaminate the pickle and leave a coating of copper on the surface of silver. To avoid this plating action use special pickle tongs and tweezers made from wood, plastic or brass. The pickle is usually kept near or next to the hearth for convenience and safety. For cleaning smaller objects and components, use a plastic sieve for immersing and retrieving work from the pickle bath.

Essentials

Lastly, the new workshop will need one or more good bench lights to focus on the work whether it is at the earliest design stage or the final polish. A strong light will help to expose any flaws or unfinished areas, which unfortunately is necessary if mistakes are to be learnt from.

The new workshop space can be a work in progress, as it is not essential to have absolutely everything set up from the word go. The basic tools and equipment that will be needed are a vice attached to solid bench, a few hammers, files, pliers and a flat plate. Obviously a hearth is essential because even objects made without soldering or construction will still need to be heated from time to time. New stakes can be expensive, so start with the essentials such as a round-topped mushroom stake and something like a bar of steel around 30mm diameter or a raising stake. Other tools can be gradually added over time, as it becomes apparent which items are being used the most. Wood can also be used for forming pressed shapes.

Most tools are steel but leather and wood are also used in the workshop.

CHAPTER 2

Working With Silver

Silver, like any natural material, has its own unique properties. It shares some characteristics with ceramic, wood or stone in that it is hard enough to be durable with sufficient strength to retain intricate shapes without the risk of collapse. Unlike those other materials, it can be melted down and recycled without changing its fundamental nature, allowing the same piece of metal to be almost endlessly reformed. This has happened throughout history, particularly at times when the monetary value of silver has increased.

Silver is rarely used in its pure form for silversmithing or jewellery as it is too soft. There are several different types of silver that are commonly used by smiths and jewellers. Copper is very soft in its annealed state so it may seem counter intuitive that its addition to silver makes it into a tougher material. The addition of a small amount of copper keeps the silver malleable but also makes it become a stronger material without noticeably affecting the colour. The long history of sterling silver comes from the fact that it has the optimal properties of durability and workability.

Sterling silver was probably first formulated in Britain as a universal standard to keep the value of coinage consistent and has long been fixed at 925 parts per thousand; this allows 7.5 per cent of copper to be present. This definition of sterling silver has existed for hundreds of years, becoming formalized to guarantee standards. Other grades of silver have also become standardized with their own different hallmarks. For the silversmith this means that the slightly purer Britannia silver has subtly different properties and its own identifiable hallmark.

Britannia silver is 958 parts silver per thousand reducing the copper content to no more than 4.2 per cent, which in turn makes the silver softer to work. This added malleability is particularly useful for techniques where there will be greater distortion or stretching of the silver, such as raising a deep vessel or an object with deeply embossed ornamentation. Britannia silver is also less likely to show the shadowy marks of copper below the surface, known as firestain.

Fine silver is virtually pure and as a result is very malleable and slightly heavier than the alloys. It will also cost more and needs to be used in a thicker sheet due to its softness. As it is not alloyed with copper there will be no chance of the firestain mentioned above. The downside is that it really is very soft, which might seem like an advantage whilst working but less so if it blemishes or dents too easily.

FIRESTAIN

Firestain is a naturally occurring patch or 'stain' of slightly darker silver where the copper trace within the sterling silver alloy becomes more obvious at the surface as a result of repeated or extended heating. A great deal of research has been done on the subject of firestain and there are three approaches to dealing with it.

Firstly, it can be avoided or minimized during production of a piece by keeping the surface of the silver protected from the air during heating, such as soldering or annealing.

Secondly, firestain can be removed with abrasive action and polished away after a piece is completed.

Lastly, firestain can be ignored as long as the entire surface is equally affected and there is no 'blotchiness' visible. This approach will result in slightly darker silver than if it were firestain-free. Historically, when there were fewer abrasives used to finish work this overall firestain would probably have been the normal colour because objects were burnished rather than mechanically buffed.

Since sterling silver is the most-used alloy of silver, it is worth knowing a little more about how to take preventative measures against firestain. These methods cannot guarantee that there will be absolutely no firestain but its likelihood is much reduced. There are two products to use; one is a specially developed powder called Argotect and the other is borax powder, which is available quite cheaply from chemists. Both powders are made up in the same way with either methylated spirits or soapy water, resulting in a thickish paste. The silver is evenly coated in a protective layer of this paste, which keeps oxygen from the surface while the work is heated during soldering or annealing.

After the process is finished the work will have to be cleaned in the acid tank as the Argotect/borax will leave a slightly 'baked on' glassy residue. This mixture should be used at the outset of a project and continued with all heating events if the aim is to stay as firestain-free as possible. It is not worth starting to use it for the last time the silver is heated if it has already been soldered or annealed many times, as the firestain will already be present. Argotect and borax will give off fumes when heated so only use this product if there is adequate ventilation or extraction. Flux for soldering contains similar compounds as it has a similar function of sealing the surface, but is used in much smaller quantities so will not produce the same amount of fumes.

HALLMARKING

Hallmarking is a stamp to prove the standard of silver. It was first recorded in the era of Emperor Augustine and was used to guarantee standards in the Byzantine era. In Britain it has existed for over 700 years and it shows the purity of sterling and other grades of silver for the purchaser. It is one of the earliest examples of customer protection in the world and it is a legal requirement for any silver object for sale to have a hallmark. There are exceptions for objects weighing less than seven grams, which excludes everything but the smallest piece of jewellery, so any silversmithing must be hallmarked if it is offered for sale. This rule applies regardless of whether the maker is a student or amateur, so if there is any intention to sell work, including online sales, it must be hallmarked.

All hallmarking is done at one of the four Assay offices, which are London, Birmingham, Sheffield and Edinburgh. A silversmith chooses which office to register with and selects a 'stamp' for their initials. This identifier confirms who has submitted the item of silver for marking. The maker's mark is followed by a purity symbol, which is traditionally a lion passant for sterling silver, although the letters '925' are now also used as an option. Each Assay office has its own specific stamp to show where the silver has been tested. The London mark is a leopard's head, the Birmingham mark is an anchor, the Sheffield mark is a Yorkshire rose and the Edinburgh mark is a castle.

Traditional marks also included a letter of the alphabet to indicate the year an object was assayed, although this is now no longer a legal requirement. Historically the assaying year ran from the 19 May, which was the feast day of the patron saint St Dunstan. Nowadays it is no longer required to have the full hallmark, so the simplified shorter choice of hallmark without a date stamp suits many jewellers because it takes up less space on the object. Most silversmiths choose to have the full number of traditional marks on their work, which generally speaking are larger objects with more space for the full mark. Hallmarks can be on the front of an object and integrated into the design. Until fairly recently, all marking was done by tapping a punch into the silver but this has changed with the development of laser marking. Punched marks can look very distinctive but there is the risk of subtle deformation of the surrounding silver, even with skilled marking. A laser mark can be of any size or depth required and as it is not delivered with a percussive blow, there is no risk of deformation of the silver. This means that an object can be finished before marking and even fragile items which include enamel can be marked without any risk of damage or distortion.

ARGENTIUM

In the 1990s a new type of silver was developed. This alloy now has its own hallmark in recognition that it has a different make-up and can be marketed as a specific silver. Argentium contains a small percentage of germanium, which replaces part of the copper trace giving the silver both firestain- and tarnish-resistant properties. It took some years of research and development by Peter Johns at Middlesex University and now Argentium silver is eligible for hallmarking at both sterling and Britannia quality, which has further established it as a choice for some smiths. Those who have adopted this innovative silver alloy tend to use it exclusively to avoid risk of contamination of tools.

Due to essential differences in its behaviour and the specific working techniques needed, use of Argentium is not covered in this book. It is sold through one supplier in the UK and they will supply fact sheets and technical material for makers wanting to try it out. Any test projects should only be done after properly studying the methodology for working Argentium as it has a few fundamental differences, which can mean a different approach to heating and soldering in particular. Always use separate tools, such as files and polishing materials that are for the sole purpose of working Argentium to avoid cross contamination with any other silver work. Argentium is not compatible with enamel but other decorative techniques are suitable. Many silversmiths who use Argentium usually stop working in the other traditional silver alloys to simplify their workshop practice and reclamation of scrap.

USING OTHER METALS

Silversmithing means that there is an inevitable expenditure on materials. To try out the techniques explored in this book, it is perfectly possible to learn everything using the cheaper alternatives of gilding metal or copper. (Brass is not suitable as it is less pliant and malleable.)

Using a substitute metal is common practice for many smiths when learning a new technique or testing an idea before committing to an expensive piece of silver. The working properties of gilding metal are designed to be very similar to those of silver and as it is cheaper, it is worth using this to start with. Copper is very soft when annealed, which can make it easy to use but it will harden fairly quickly once it is worked. It is easy to order a piece of sheet copper online or even recycle an old boiler, as these are usually made from copper. The thickness of copper from boilers is somewhat less than is ideal for techniques like raising at around 0.7mm, but this is fine for trial efforts and test projects.

Some of the following projects do not have strictly defined measurements because there will be circumstances where the size of a project is determined by the available tools. For those makers used to creating objects in other materials, they will have the advantage of visualizing sizes. Copper and gilding metal are ideal for experimentation and trial runs because they allow a smith to familiarize themselves with scale, volume, dimension and sizes in general. It is important to work in millimetres rather than centimetres because this will ensure the best level of accuracy and to remember the old saying, 'measure twice, cut once'. Most of the projects can be made with 1mm sheet silver, though there will be instances where that is not quite strong enough. Working with slightly thinner sheet is easier once some experience has been gained with the material.

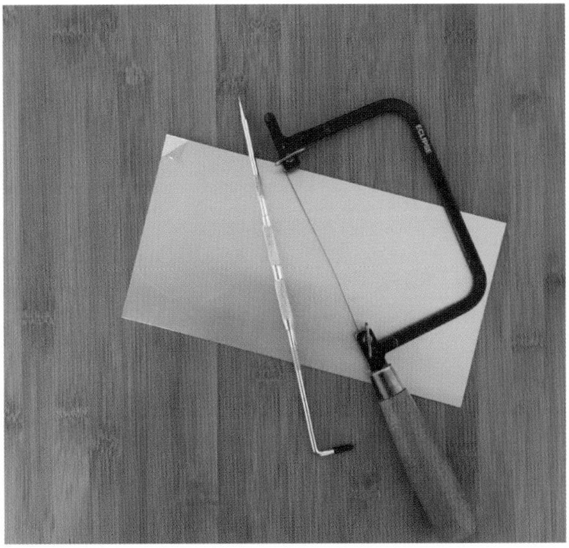

Silver sheet, some with a protective plastic covering, and copper for trials.

CHAPTER 3

Design and Decoration

What is the purpose of design and why is it important? We live in a visually enriched world with images of beauty and ingenuity just one click away. Some might be tempted to ask why not take an image 'off the shelf' instead of labouring over something new, especially if drawing an original idea seems a daunting task. Apart from the morally dubious aspect of stealing designs, it will not help to expand anyone's knowledge. It is definitely worth studying the work of those who have produced beautiful examples of silversmithing and contemplating where inspiration may have come from, but in the end it is important to try to make an object of your own.

When faced with the enormity of a blank page, the whole business of design can seem impossible to visualize. Whilst there may be no shortage of ideas and sources of inspiration, it can be hard to translate this onto paper then to be magically turned into silver reality.

Amongst the many misconceptions around what design is and what it is for is the notion that design is only on the surface. Design most certainly is about the visual appearance of an object and this does include the surface, either ornamented or not, but that is only part of the story. Design begins with the technique being employed to make an item. Decisions about the form and its appearance will also be influenced by how the object is to be used. Spending time thinking about how an object is used will raise questions, such as will it need a handle or does it sit on a surface? A good designer needs to address these matters as well consider the best method to produce a beautiful object.

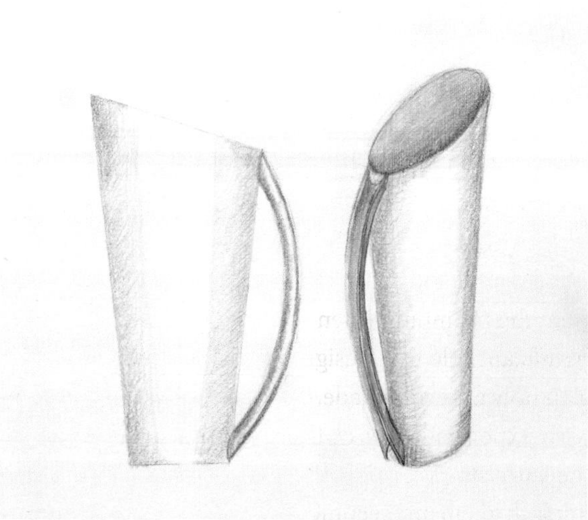

Drawing and shading to create dimension.

Silversmithing is all about creating something that may have a function, but must be special. The tactile and aesthetic qualities must be examined beyond those merely practical features and the balance, weight and scale should be resolved in advance when precious time and materials are being invested in the project. In other words, it is not just the visual but also the practical and sensual considerations which have to be included

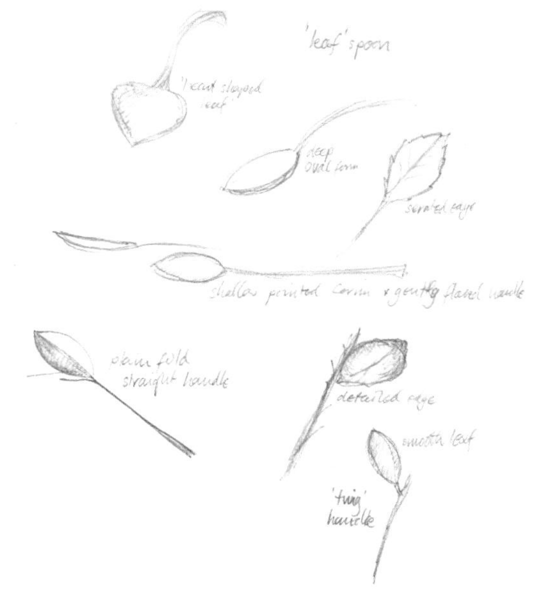

Getting first ideas on paper.

from the beginning when working in metal. The other significant role that design plays is that it will help to plan how a piece is made. This will become instinctive with experience but at the outset of designing and the early stages of learning to work metal, it helps to think through any technical limitations in advance. In particular, where there are several different techniques in the production of an item, design can help work out which steps to take first and how to proceed next.

When designing three-dimensional objects, it helps enormously to gain basic understanding of how something is made and why it is constructed in that way. First efforts at design will not be the same as those ideas that come from the results of time spent at the workbench when there is more experience to draw on. A novice silversmith will need to discover the possibilities of a technique and learn how to unlock the potential of the metal. Experiments with base metal such as copper or gilding metal can demonstrate fairly quickly what is viable and pleasing. After trying out some tests and trials it is time to return to the drawing board and allow this new-found knowledge to guide the creative process. The first projects in this book are focused on simple techniques to get started with making and can be revisited any number of times with a view to taking the aesthetic possibilities further.

DRAWING YOUR DESIGN

Drawing is important for design because this is the chance to theorize at each stage. Some people wrongly assume that they cannot design because they do not draw particularly well, but it is possible to learn a few simple techniques to get started. Good draughtsmanship may not come naturally but will improve with practice, so do not let a fear of drawing be a deterrent to trying. It is important to remember that these drawings are not for anybody to admire as works of art but instead are part of a work in progress. One of the difficulties with expressing ideas for a three-dimensional object is that drawing is a two-dimensional medium and it may not fully express what the designer wishes to achieve. This is where model making as an additional approach to design can help to give a more accurate guide to the physical properties of an object in its three-dimensional form.

Design for silversmithing works best with a combination of different types of drawing, model making where possible, tests in base metal and then a final design. Rough sketches to start will help to determine the basics for overall shape. A more accurate scale drawing can then be used to determine the finer points such as exact dimensions and type of polish or hammered finish. Finally, model making in card or paper followed by simple trials in copper or gilding metal can help decide whether the principal will work. At this stage, some aspects of the original idea may have been thrown out and replaced by other versions. In this way the final design can be arrived at in an unforced way, allowing ideas to evolve and develop.

Models can help determine scale and proportion.

To get started, make sure that all of the usual drawing tools are to hand; paper, pencils, ruler, compass, circle template, small square or protractor, and a curves template. Most of the projects in this book will probably fit onto size A4 paper but A3 has the advantage of allowing several sketches to a page for the purpose of comparison. For model making use either graph paper, which is great as it has measurements marked on the surface, or thin card, which has the advantage of rigidity. Models do not need to be sophisticated to help with the design development. Indeed a quickly taped-together model can help to determine any thoughts about proportion that are hard to visualize in two dimensions. Constructing a few options can help with both the final idea and provide a useful template for making the piece.

The other essentials are scissors or cutting blade and mat, instant paper adhesive and masking tape.

Small ideas sketches are fine as a form of visual note-taking but draw all the final design ideas to scale. This means the same size as the proposed object so that it can be compared once the making begins. Remember that creating a drawing to scale will also be a chance to check that there are the correct tools for the job. Don't go planning something when there is no means of making it with the equipment available unless there is a way to make dedicated tooling. Start drawing with a soft pencil to get a feel for the right line and once refined, go over with a fine or medium marker pen for a bold and easy-to-see outline. It doesn't matter if the first idea is not right, it's only a drawing. Working on paper to produce multiple sketches will eventually lead to the right proportions and this is where a design idea will start to coalesce. Many projects may only need an outline in the first instance but remember that as a three-dimensional object there will be measurements of depth that account for the full expression of the form. A 'rendered' drawing is one that has been given the appearance of a three-dimensional form with shading and tonal work to emphasize the sense of depth. Rendering will also help to visualize how a finished object can look. It is good practice to get into the habit of noting down measurements on the design to show exactly how long, how wide and deep a piece is to be. This information will be essential when making up a list of materials needed.

Dimensions and proportions are just one aspect of the design that may be in part dictated by the tools available. This is an aspect of design as it falls into that area of preparation that has to be considered at the outset. It is no good designing an object without the means to produce it. For those with access to the

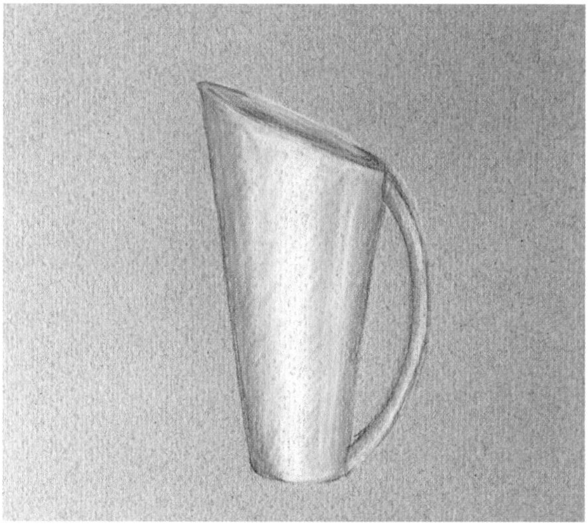

A rendered drawing helps to visualize a design.

right equipment or skills, it is possible to make tools. Without such knowledge it is still possible to find a way of working which uses tools in a different way. This all means experimentation. Playing about with materials and equipment can lead to inspiration.

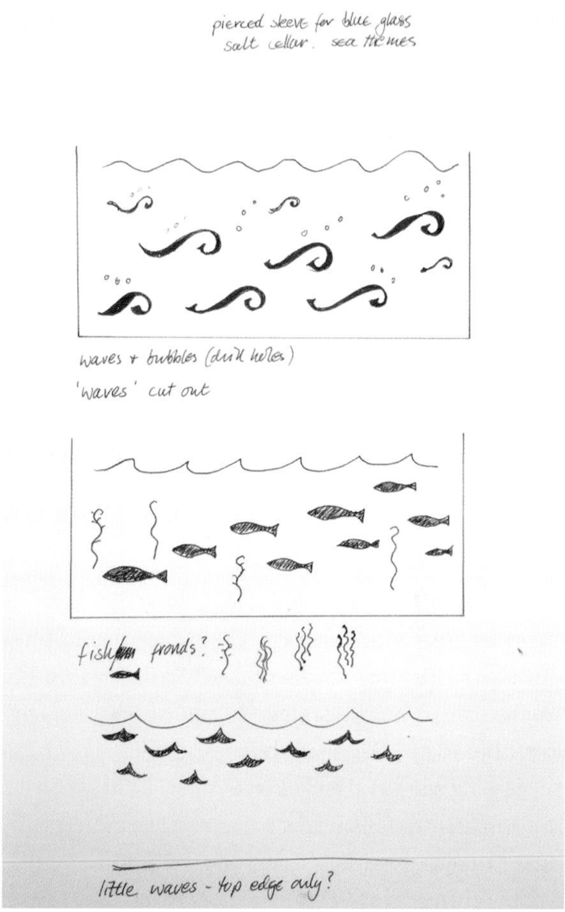

Designing and planning a pierced out design.

CHOOSING A FINISH

After deciding on the size and shape of an object, its surface finish should be considered. Silver lends itself particularly well to a range of different possibilities; it can be highly polished, patterned or textured, pale or oxidized, matt or satin. These are the features that cannot be captured in a card or paper model, but copper trials can help to determine the finish even though it is a different colour. Copper models will also take the design further into the technical realm where each of the basic steps of construction can be tested and resolved before working in silver.

The different projects will each have their own design possibilities and most techniques can be elegantly employed to decorative ends. Well-controlled hammering or planishing leaves a beautiful surface that catches the light, needing little further in embellishment. The choice of shape and finish may provide enough in terms of design but there are instances where surface development can be taken much further. A design will provide the profile and desired 'mood' of a piece, but if surface ornamentation is required then the design moves into new territory where decoration is used to enhance visible surfaces. Many structural elements can be employed decoratively, such as piercing. If there is any part of a piece that calls for some openwork or cut-out areas then this is an opportunity to employ design to enhance an object in which the need already existed for some cut-away area. Piercing can add refined details and depth to an otherwise simple object.

Cellular patterns, whether crisp geometric shapes or fluid abstract forms inspired by nature, can be achieved very efficiently through this fairly simple technique. It is worth mentioning that if sawing is to be used, it should be designed so that it can be executed without damaging any other part of the work with enough clearance for the movement of the saw.

CHASING AND REPOUSSE

Chasing and its companion repousse are amongst the most ancient techniques for decoration and have been practiced in some way for as long as objects have been made in metal. No material is removed in these techniques, just gently pushed into low relief. Roughly speaking, chasing is used to create impressed lines that are tapped into the metal with a tool from the front surface. The chasing tool bears some similarity to a little chisel, but as it is smooth it glides over the surface rather than gouging into it. Chasing can be used on its own for shallow linear and textural designs or for creating a different depth but it is frequently used with repousse where metal is pushed out from the opposite side to create greater contouring. Both methods of ornamentation are done using punch tools. The punches are ground into a variety of shapes at the end and polished to a high shine so that the point of contact imparts no unintentional blemishes onto the surface of the metal. A wide-faced repousse hammer is used to tap the punch tool across the supported surface of the metal and provides enough pressure to leave an indentation. This hammer has evolved to provide a fairly light feel in the hand so that it can be used for long periods of time, but provides enough pressure to move or push the sheet of silver. The end of the handle has a rounded bulbous shape to fit in the hand comfortably while the shaft is slender and springy. The hammer head has a very wide, flat face for striking the punches and a neat, small ball pein on the other end for direct forming of sheet metal.

A snow leopard by Bryony Knox on chasing pitch with tools.

In order for a pattern to be pushed out, the work must be supported on a softer surface than the normal steel of an anvil or stake. The traditional material for this is pitch, which is mixed up when molten at a low temperature and poured into a cast iron bowl or solid tray. There are various recipes for pitch, which must have the property of some 'give' when the metal is punched but also be resistant enough that the punch can do no damage or puncture the surface of the metal. Usually, pitch is made up of tar with some plaster to provide the material with body or density, and resin and tallow to make it slightly more plastic.

Chasing and repousse tools can be made from thin steel rod or very thick 6in nails, filed and polished to the required shape. Ideally the steel should be hardened so that the tools don't buckle under the pressure of repeated hammering. Different shapes are used to create different marks or hollows, such as straight edges for tracing lines and more rounded ones for pushing out larger areas.

This technique is very attractive for surface ornamentation and suitable for use on a wide range of objects. It can be very messy to use but is well worth experimenting with in copper. Taking a short course is an ideal way to sample a new technique such as this, where special tools and materials are needed.

ENGRAVING

Engraving is a decorative technique where fine 'v' shaped grooves are carved into the surface of the metal with a small hand-held tool. It is unlike chasing because the surface of the metal is incised and a small curl of metal is scraped away. Looking at an engraved piece of metal, it is possible to see the sheen of cleanly cut lines as they flow across the surface. Machine engraving does not have quite the same appearance because the cutters do not have the same crisp line of a finely hand-engraved mark. The hand-held engraving tool has to be sharp, with the working edge sharpened at the correct angle for accurate cutting that neither skids across the surface nor gouges into it. Engraving takes a great deal of practice to learn but the time spent will pay dividends. As this is a specialist skill that takes years to perfect, it is worth looking for short courses to get started so that the proper technique is learned from the outset.

Engraving tools.

ETCHING

Etching may not be as ancient as the other mark-making methods of ornamenting a surface of metal but it is worth mentioning. It is not particularly complicated to do but because acid is employed in the removal of the metal, there are health and safety considerations. Chemical etching occurs when a 'mordant' that is an acid or other substance 'eats' away at areas of exposed metal. The word 'mordant' comes from the French and means 'to bite', which perfectly describes the minutely nibbled appearance of etching. The most commonly used and best mordant for etching silver is dilute nitric acid, although it is possible with other substances. A design or pattern is achieved when the unornamented areas of the surface are protected by a lacquer, stopping-out varnish or wax, known as the 'resist'. The exposed metal is then dissolved away when the object is immersed in the mordant, creating a design on the metal. Great care has to be taken with the preparation of the metal surface so that only the designated design or pattern is exposed to the acid. The protective resist must also be used to seal the back and sides of the metal so that it is not inadvertently exposed.

During etching the piece should be checked regularly so that it does not dissolve too fast and end up ruining a carefully prepared design. As silver is etched away it bubbles around the immediate area of exposure and a small residue of waste material can build up on the surface, which should be brushed away so that there is no interference with the etch continuing to work. Traditionally a feather is used to brush the etching surface to keep it clear. This is because a feather is unaffected by the action of the acid and is soft enough for the resist to remain undamaged.

The traditional method of etching described above has been enhanced with the highly accurate use of photographic images in photo etching. The etching part is the same but it is the application of the design to the silver with a light-sensitive coating for the resist that differs from the hand-applied version. The process

Silver book box by Vicky Ambery Smith with photoetching by Mary Ann Simmons.

requires a photo lab and an old-fashioned dark room, which is why smiths who use this technique send their work to a specialist who can provide this service. By outsourcing the etching, all that is needed is good-quality artwork for a guaranteed high quality end result.

The main problem with undertaking etching in a small workshop is the storage and ultimate disposal of the nitric acid. Due to these difficulties, it is worth looking for dedicated etching forums on the internet who can put makers in touch with any local workshops offering demonstrations or trials.

ENAMELLING

Enamelling is a beautiful embellishment to silver and has a long history of bringing colour to otherwise monochrome objects. Expertise with enamels developed around a thousand years ago, with the city of Limoges in central France becoming a famed centre for the production of enamelled religious artefacts. Enamel is ground-up particles of coloured glass which, when heated to melting point, will fuse onto the metal surface to create a glossy layer of colour. This description makes enamelling sound fairly easy and in essence all that is required is a freshly cleaned surface of copper or silver, freshly prepared enamel and a reliable heat source to fuse the glass onto its background. Of course nothing is ever that simple and the difference between getting enamel to melt and stick to a surface is one thing; it is entirely another for it to be truly exquisite.

Having said that, enamelling is fairly easy to experiment with as it can be heated at the hearth on a tripod without the expense of buying a kiln. The main difficulty with using enamel is the need for fastidiously clean silver and a working area where no dust or contamination can get onto an unfired surface.

Opaque enamel as the name suggests is solid colour that does not allow the metal below to show through. Although translucent colours sound as if they are somewhat diluted, the colours are in fact rich and intense. Many enamellers combine translucent colours with other texturing techniques so that the shimmer of an engraved line or patterned hollow shows off the full richness of the pigment. Enamels melt at around the same temperature as hard solder, which means that objects created with areas of enamelling will need to be made either with enamelling solder or assembled in some other way.

RESIN

Resin is a two-part liquid plastic that can be pigmented to be either opaque or translucent and is fixed with a drop of setting agent. Because it is fairly runny before it is fully cured, it is only suitable for enclosed hollow areas and can be used for inclusions such as silver dust or crumbs of gold leaf for decorative effect. Cold enamel is a variant of this type of material, but it is nearer to true enamel in that it tends to be used as a thinner layer of pigment that can be fired in the domestic oven to cure it. Both resin and cold enamel are fairly easy to experiment with and there are various kits on the market that include all the materials needed

Cara Murphy's enamelled bubble bowls.

for experimentation. As both of these are plastic-type materials, any soldering and construction would be completed before using these for finishing touches or adding colour to an object.

Other surface decoration can be achieved through impressing or imprinting, using a rolling mill to create a patterned piece of sheet to use as a detail in an object. The rolling mill is an excellent way to create roller-printed surface patterns but is somewhat limited for large areas unless the rollers are wide, which rules out all but the most expensive mills.

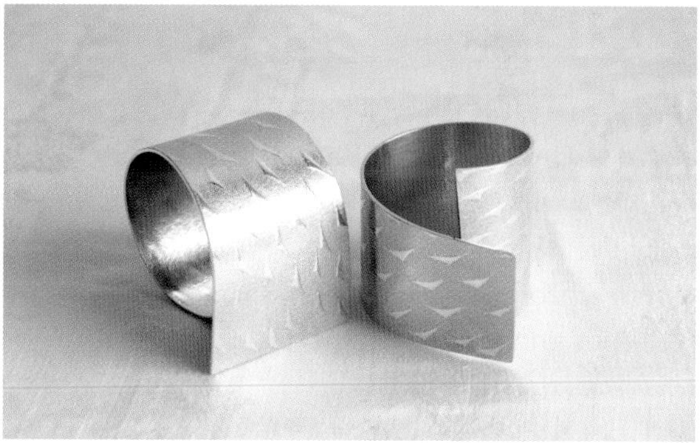

Roller printed napkin rings.

FORGING AND RAISING

Forging is one of those techniques that is both structural and beautifully decorative at the same time. The process creates sweeping, dynamic lines well suited to sculptural forms and offers all sorts of design possibilities. It allows the raw material to be brought to life and added surface decoration may not be needed when the lines of formed silver speak for themselves. Raising, like forging, is one of the hammered construction methods that can also define a design without the need for any further embellishment. The silhouette alone as the defining aspect of a design can be traced back to the highly influential Danish silversmith Georg Jensen. This approach to using fluid and dynamic lines was developed over 100 years ago and it has never really fallen out of favour, in spite of changing tastes over the years. This is probably due to those fundamental elements of form, balance, space and their relationship.

Design is therefore so much more than a beautiful idea; it is how to realize those inspirational thoughts and anticipate any potential problems along the way. Design for silversmithing should draw together the visual and the technical to guide the smith from first idea to completed object and will get easier with the accumulation of knowledge and expertise.

CHAPTER 4

Hammering Techniques – Sinking and Planishing

Forming and changing metal with a hammer is probably the oldest continually used technique in silversmithing.

Flat sheet can be transformed into three-dimensional shapes just by clever use of hammering on an anvil or steel flat plate. Gaining skill with a hammer is absolutely central to silversmithing and although there are other ways to form metal, this simple technology can be incredibly sophisticated. The shape of a hammer head will determine how metal can be shaped, distorted and extended. Flat sheet metal will stretch when struck with a hammer and by exploiting this property, three-dimensional shapes can be created.

Sinking is one of the easiest methods to introduce depth into an otherwise flat piece of metal. It is not suitable for really deep vessels but is very quick and effective for shallow bowls.

SINKING

Sinking is used to create fairly shallow concave or convex forms, so is an ideal hammering technique for new silversmiths to learn. It lends itself perfectly to making dishes or bowls. The only dimension which will change during sinking is the depth of a piece, not the outline or circumference. Sinking works because the rounded end of a ball pein hammer is squashing the metal outwards in all directions as it strikes the surface. Each hammer blow from a ball pein will spread the metal in 360 degrees from the point of contact. Keeping the hammer blows overlapping within an area will create an even expansion of the metal. The outer edge of the cut-out disc is never hammered so it will not stretch whereas the hammered inner area will, meaning the expanding centre will have to bulge or push outwards. This method of working is done from the concave/hollow inside of the bowl with a steel flat plate underneath. Constant hammering will harden the metal, so make sure that the silver is annealed once the surface has been hammered all over. The project below can be based on a simple circle or other outline shapes such as an oval or asymmetric outline, which makes it a very versatile method of shallow forming. To begin with try this on a circular blank, just to get a feel for what is happening to the metal.

The 'blank' is the name used for unformed cut-out sheet. After working out the design dimensions, these will have to be transferred to the surface of the metal.

Silver comes from the bullion dealer with a protective plastic film. It is possible to scratch the outline through this surface with a sharp scriber, but if this fine line is not easy to see then try a thin marker pen on the plastic surface. An alternative is to peel off the plastic and cover the metal with masking tape. This is a good surface to draw on with either a biro or fine-tipped marker pen. The tape can be left in place until the shape has been cut out and is ready to use. To avoid any snags or roughness, give the edges a quick file after sawing out.

Start hammering with the round ball pein end, working about 5mm from the outer edge. Keep hammering round, gradually working towards the centre until the whole area apart from the outer 5mm rim is evenly worked. A larger bowl is harder to control so to minimize any distortion, alternate the direction of hammering each round. By working in a clockwise then anticlockwise direction, the pressure applied is more likely to be even throughout the whole area of metal. Make sure to overlap the hammer blows so that there are no obvious gaps or ridges. This is easier to see by turning the metal over to look at the back and see if there are any voids or unworked patches. Even with neatly hammered work the piece may not yet look as expected, but do not worry – this is a gradual process and small uneven parts can be corrected at each stage.

Sinking a bowl.

ANNEALING

Annealing is heating metal to reduce the stress or pressure of being worked, thereby restoring its malleability. With all shaping, hammering and stretching techniques, silver will become work-hardened. This is the natural result of the continual compression that happens during many metalworking processes. To restore the flexibility or malleability of the metal it must be annealed before continuing to work it.

If silver is not annealed after a round of hammering, it will feel very resistant and hard but could also become damaged by metal fatigue. This is because the metal when cool has a crystalline structure. Overworking the silver without regular annealing breaks up the structure and the metal can crack or fracture. Although theoretically possible to heat any cracks to the point of melting together, it is not a reliable method of 'mending' damaged metal. Just make sure not to hammer the same area over and over and to anneal it once the whole surface has been worked.

When metal is annealed, it is taken to a temperature lower than melting point but the heat is such that the crystals can start to reconfigure. Rapid quenching in cold water stops this process in its tracks before the crystalline structure is too neatly arranged and there are still some gaps between the cell-like crystals. It is this slightly irregular arrangement with many microscopic gaps or 'vacancies' that allows the silver to be malleable once more. Theoretically the crystals will continue to align themselves into a more ordered structure over time – however, this need not be a concern as the process is extremely slow. Under normal circumstances, metal will not become hardened unless it has been worked or manipulated in some way so it will not become hard if put away and left untouched for a period of time.

The same rules apply for working with copper, gilding metal or silver. However, copper is very soft after annealing but hardens more quickly than silver while it is being worked. Gilding metal is alloyed to give it very similar working properties to silver so it hardens more gradually.

To anneal silver/copper/gilding metal, make sure the hearth area is large enough to accommodate the piece and that there is water nearby to dunk it in immediately after heating. As explained above, quenching is part of the process. Check the work is safely positioned on the hearth so that it can be heated as quickly and evenly as possible. Heat hollow objects from the outside/convex side so that the flame can flow over the surface and will not 'blow back'. Learning to judge the temperature of annealing is very important and may take some practice. If possible dim the lights or close the blinds to make the colour changes in the hot metal more visible. The right temperature has to be achieved for the softening to take place. Not enough heat will result in an item that is unannealed or still work-hardened. If the silver is overheated it can damage the surface and it could harden the metal by allowing the crystal structure to become too regular and therefore too dense. Overheated metal can crack when worked.

Quenching the metal in water is essential so always keep tongs or tweezers readily to hand. It is useful to clean work in pickle after heating because the dilute sulphuric acid will whiten the silver, making future hammering easy to see against the matt white background. Always rinse and dry the work thoroughly before continuing.

Practise annealing copper to get used to finding the right temperature and gain confidence with the gas torch before working in silver.

A consequence of repeated or extended heating is firestain – this is covered in Chapter 2.

PLANISHING AND CAULKING

These are techniques to finish off formed metal. Planishing is used to flatten out previous hammer marks and can be left as the final surface or as a preparation before filing and polishing. A planishing hammer does not need to be heavy but should have an almost flat, very highly polished face so that no marks are transferred to the surface. Hammer blows are kept tightly overlapped to create the smoothest finish possible and this can be taken right to the edge, so that the whole surface is planished. Planishing is done from the outside of the object, which is supported on a rounded stake of a suitable profile. Stakes come in all shapes and sizes to accommodate all potential curves and hollows, so make sure that the profile is a good fit to the shape of the work. The stake does not have to match the profile exactly just as long as the object can have contact at the point where it is hammered. It may be necessary to anneal the piece and planish it again to ensure that the inner surface is thoroughly smoothed.

As with all steel tools, keep stakes away from moisture and lightly oil after use if the workshop is prone to dampness. Rust can pit the surface of tools and like the planishing hammer a smooth, polished stake will contribute to the finish of an object.

As the surfaces are smoothed out by hammering, so can the edges be treated with a final hammering. This is used alongside other techniques and is specifically for adding a finishing touch to a rim or top edge. It can be done after any filing or abrasives have been used. Support the work on a sandbag so that the object is sitting edge-up and can be lightly tapped with a hammer. A planishing hammer is ideal for most edges, or a hammer with a slightly concave face. The effect is one that is subtly shimmering and it adds an attractive detail to a finished object. Caulking is often used on cups and vessels to give the appearance of a thicker edge. Caulking can also be used more frequently during the creation of hammered objects to stop edges becoming thinned during the making process. An alternative to the subtle edge is a more pronounced pattern and this is done with a ball pein or cross pein hammer, which will leave little indents around the edge.

FILING

The file is made so that the 'cutting' action works when the file is pushed away. A medium or 2-cut file will remove unwanted metal fairly quickly if the full length of the file is used in a long, sweeping movement. The file is removing metal so always watch the progress carefully and if the cut is too coarse for the job in hand, change to a smoother one such as a cut 4.

ABRASIVES AND BURNISHING

The inner and outer surfaces can be left with the hammered finish but the top edge has been filed and will need to be smoothed to remove the small grooves or file marks. This is done with emery sticks. They can be bought ready-made as a set but it is easy to make some with a 20–30cm lengths of flat wood and different grades of emery securely taped in place. They are used like a file and make quick work of removing file or hammer marks ready for a final polish.

The burnisher is a smooth steel tool about the size of a pen and is rubbed over a surface to smooth it for a final polish. In the days before there were lots of different polishing materials, most silver had a burnished surface. Burnishers have also been made of agate. They work best with some lubrication for a 'spit and polish' finish. It is not necessary to spit on the work, just lick the back of a hand and use a small amount of saliva to help the smooth tool slide over the surface being worked. Take care doing this as some burnishers have a sharp point and a misdirected movement can leave a scratch. Burnishing can be used on emeried edges for a shiny finish or caulked edges for additional sparkle.

DESIGN POSSIBILITIES

This simple, shallow dish can be made as a round bowl, but this is not an essential requirement for the technique as it can be applied to a variety of outlines. It is not particularly well suited to creating crisp corners so it is best to avoid shapes that do not have a rounded profile. The example below is for a small, circular dish. If this first project feels too modest the same technique can be applied to something much larger. However, with a greater diameter comes more hammering and more opportunity for temporary distortion. After the first hammering it can appear as if the shape is losing its way and the bowl starts to look like a Pringle or taco, taking on a 'u' shape rather than an even hollow. If this happens, anneal the piece and place it upside-down at the edge of the tree trunk or workbench and mallet the edge down, focusing on the uneven areas first. Turn the bowl so that all points around the edge are eventually pushed down by the mallet. When turned the right way round, the shape will be much nearer to its intended form and the project can continue. It is not unusual to have to right a shape during the making process, so it is important to learn how and when to use the mallet to keep the project on track.

Health and safety

There are few health and safety issues with this project but keep fingers safe when sawing and hammering. Keep a firm grip on the object while it is being worked as this is safer and less likely to result in any wobbles. If there are any miss-hits where the edge of the planishing hammer leaves an unwanted dent, it can be worked over around the problem area to remove or minimize the mark. Always remember to grip the end of the handle of the hammer; that way there is maximum effect for minimum effort.

This is principally a hammering project, so wear ear defenders.

SINKING AND PLANISHING PROJECT

Make a small dish for a tea strainer.

Tools

- Engineer's dividers or compass for a circular dish or
- Engineer's scribe and template for an asymmetrical or non-circular dish
- Ball pein hammer
- Planishing hammer
- Steel flat plate
- Steel mushroom stake or similar
- Wood or rawhide mallet
- Emery sticks of grades 240–1,000
- Burnisher

Materials

- Silver, copper or gilding metal 0.9mm thick 50–70mm. For a bigger bowl, use thicker silver of 1mm or more.

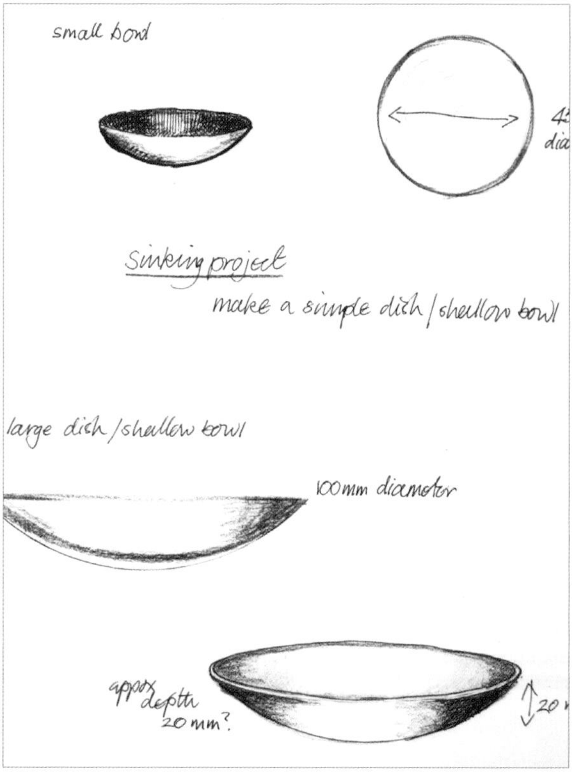

STEP 1 Draw the design for the dish including both a plan (top down view) and side elevation (a cross section showing the desired depth). The work can be compared to the drawing as it progresses.

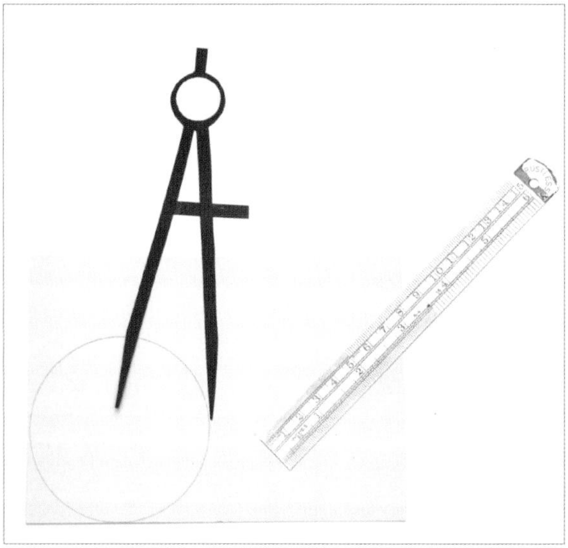

STEP 2 Transfer the design onto the metal. Either scratch through the plastic coating onto the metal with dividers or draw onto the film or masking tape with a pen.

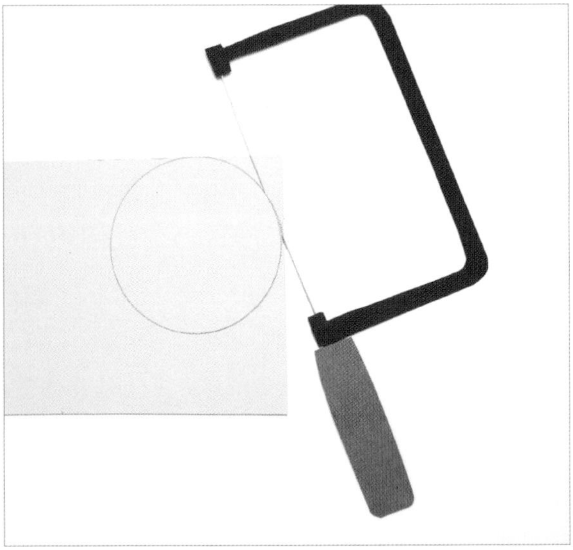

STEP 3 Saw out the silver with a piercing saw. If this is a first attempt at sawing, start at a slight angle to make an initial cut then keep working the saw vertically. Don't worry about breaking a blade; practice makes perfect.

STEP 4 Mark circle guidelines on the metal to keep the hammering even and restricted to an area within 5mm from the outer edge. All of the hammering will happen inside this area meaning that the edge will not be struck or stretched.

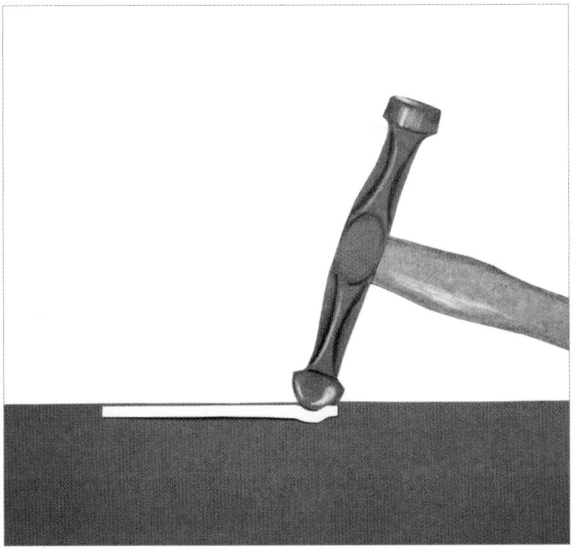

STEP 5 Place the cut-out disc on the steel flat plate and hammer from the outer circle with a ball pein hammer. Hold the disc so it is in contact with the flat surface while it is being hammered. Hammer just inside the outer edge of the circle.

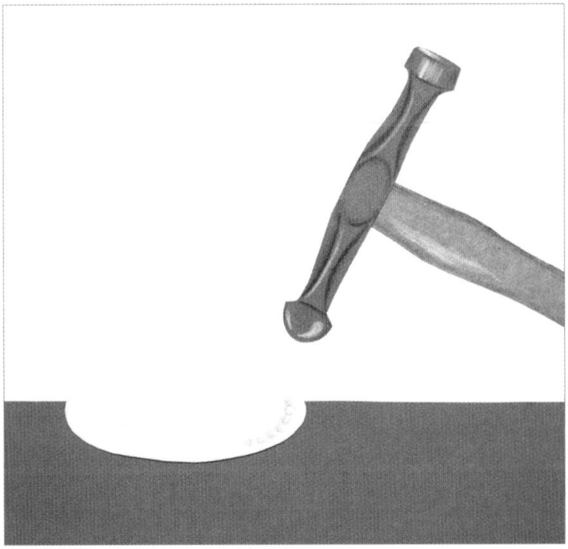

STEP 6 Continue hammering the first circle. Avoiding the outer edge, keep the hammer blows tightly packed together. After the first circle, continue round without any gaps. Hammering can be done between the circles, which are for guidance.

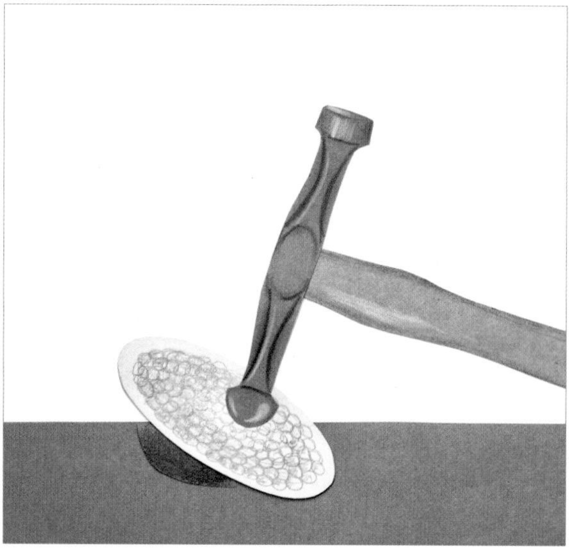

STEP 7 As more of the surface becomes deformed by the hammering it will be necessary to hold the disc at an angle. This is to keep the hammering in contact with the steel flat plate. Cover the whole disc with neat, overlapping hammer blows.

STEP 8 Anneal the disc to restore its softness or malleability. Place it on a firebrick, convex side outwards. The hot part of the flame is the softer darker-blue colour and this is aimed at the work to heat it. Stop when the whole surface reaches a dull red colour and quench the metal in cold water.

STEP 9 After cleaning, rinsing and drying the metal, the sinking can be repeated to create a deeper form. When deep enough, planish the annealed dish on a round/ mushroom stake held in the vice. Keep the dish in contact with the stake at the point where it is being planished.

STEP 10 Planish the whole surface and check that it satisfactory. It can be annealed and planished again if it has become too hard to work.

STEP 11 This piece is left with a planished finish. The edge can be emeried and then burnished smooth or it can be lightly hammered for a textured edge.

This first project is an introduction to basic metal forming. It is a chance to find out how metal can be deformed, stretched and controlled in a predictable manner. Although a simple technique, it can be used on any scale as the central premise remains the same. To work on a larger form, always start with a thicker gauge of copper or silver because sinking will thin the metal somewhat. Sinking can be used in lots of other projects where a gently domed form is needed, such as a curved lid or softly hollowed area. After trying this technique on a small scale for a little dish for a tea strainer, try it on a larger diameter disc for a shallow bonbon bowl.

CHAPTER 5

Doming, Drilling and Soldering

Many objects are made using a combination of techniques. Individually these pose few problems but when put together it is important to know in what order to do each step of the project. Curved forms may need to join flat parts and three-dimensional forms may include cut-out areas of piercing for decorative or structural purposes. Knowing what to do in advance will make the transition from design to finished object much more straightforward. The example below uses a combination of three basic skills to make something special, with lots of potential for design development.

Tea strainer project.

In this project there will be a three-dimensional form made using a doming block. Unlike sinking in the previous chapter where a shallow dish is made with many hammer blows onto a flat surface, this method uses a punch and mallet to push the flat sheet into a formed hollow of steel or wood. When an object needs to have holes drilled into the surface it is easier and safer to do this when the object is still flat sheet. However, complex designs or patterns can be difficult to plan because of the potential for distortion that occurs when flat sheet is pressed into a hollow. Round holes will become somewhat oval or stretched when the flat disc is pushed into the hollow former to make a domed form. The holes can be left as ovals or made round after doming with a hand-held point such as a scriber.

Roughly speaking, if the piece has holes in it then it is preferable to drill into a flat surface because this is easier and much safer. To guarantee that the holes are perfectly positioned use a centre punch to tap a little dent for each hole. The centre punch provides a visual marker for positioning the drill, so it won't slip or go off course. If the plan is to use the drilled holes as a starting point for cut-out shapes, just make a drill hole and leave any sawing till later. Never pierce out a design until the object is fully formed into its final three-dimensional shape. This is because the cut-out areas of the sheet offer no resistance while being shaped and will expand leaving parts of the metal unformed and very distorted, thus spoiling the design. In other words, cut-out designs on a three-dimensional form are done last after the forming is completed.

There may be occasions when an object has to be drilled after forming and in such an instance it is possible to drill into a curved surface from the inside. However it is awkward to do because the bowl form must be held absolutely perpendicular to the drill. This can be dangerous because it is difficult to hold an object that is not flat. It is strongly recommended that for this project, the holes are drilled when the sheet is still flat and unformed, regardless of whether they are going to be used for a pierced-out design or just left as holes.

This project introduces silver soldering to join the handles to the rounded body of the bowl. The handles must be filed to fit the outline of the bowl properly so that there are no spaces, because silver solder is used to join pieces but not fill gaps. The steps below show soldering with 'paillons' or snippets of solder in position. This is a typical jewellery technique but is suitable for a first go at soldering because the contact areas are small and it will allow a novice to see how the process works. Solder will always flow as soon as the right temperature is achieved, so watch the work while it is being heated and see that the temperature is the same on either side of the join. Solder will reach a molten state very quickly once the surrounding metal is hot enough. Move the flame away and switch off the heat as soon as this happens. The work can be picked up with reverse-action tweezers and quenched straight away. The silver will cool instantly; it may not be possible to inspect the soldered seam until traces of flux have been removed so place the tea strainer in the pickle to clean for a few moments.

All that remains is to tidy up with emery and polish. One of the problems that can arise during soldering is that the flux bubbles up when first exposed to the heat of the torch. If the snippets of solder are displaced then switch off the gas and reposition them with fine tweezers. If the flux bubbles up and displaces to the two parts to be joined, hold the flame aside and gently nudge them back into contact with the reverse-action tweezers before continuing to heat the work. All soldering depends on preparation, contact and both parts being joined reaching the right temperature together. The handles are smaller so can heat more quickly. Allow the flame to build heat on the domed part before aiming the torch at the handle and actual seam area.

DESIGN POSSIBILITIES

A tea strainer has a fairly simple function; it must sit on top of a cup or mug to catch tea leaves, whilst tea is poured into the vessel below. This determines the basic parameters for the design; a hollow form or small bowl to catch the tea leaves, holes for the tea to flow through without the leaves escaping into the cup and one or two handles to support the piece. The holes can be arranged in a pattern, be of slightly different sizes or used as the starting point for some intricate piercing. The handles can both be the same or one short and the other longer – either way this is another design opportunity for making something unique.

Health and safety

When using the drill always wear safety goggles to protect against flying scraps of metal. Keep hair and clothing well away from any machinery. The centre-punched dent will stop the drill bit skidding on the surface but if it is not possible to make a preliminary mark, then drill through masking tape as this will also work. The object being drilled must be clamped down or held firmly while the drill is in motion. If there is any problem with the drilling, switch off and unplug before sorting it out. Drilling into an old chunk of wood will support the flat sheet but constant re-drilling will leave a hollow, so change the position of the wood from time to time. Again – just another reminder – always wear safety goggles when drilling.

SILVER TEA STRAINER

Tools

- Dividers or template for marking a circle
- Piercing saw to cut out the 'blank'
- Half-round hand file to smooth the edges
- Centre punch and steel flat plate for accurately marking the drill holes
- A small bench drill
- Sandbag or shallow wooden former
- Doming block and large punch or large ball pein hammer
- Large mallet
- Emery papers in various grades
- Polishing cloth and compounds

Materials

- Sheet silver circle for the bowl 0.7mm thick, between 45mm–65mm diameter
- Silver sheet or thick wire for the handles/support

STEP 1 Sketch out ideas to scale and work out the details such as the size of the hollow part (45–65mm) and the handles dimension. Then select the tools for this project.

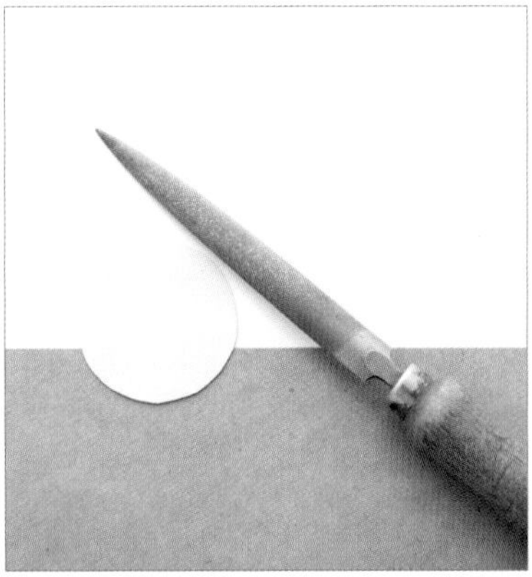

STEP 2 Mark out the disc for the bowl section, and saw it out. File the blank circle so the shape is regular and the edges smooth.

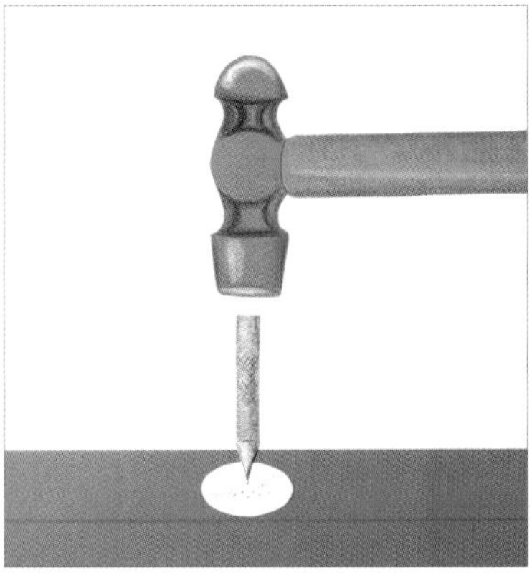

STEP 3 Hold the silver on a steel flat plate and mark the site of each hole. Tap the centre punch with a mallet to make a tiny dent ready for drilling.

STEP 4 Check the size of drill bit, line it up with the first hole and hold firmly while bringing the drill down. Drill all the holes as marked.

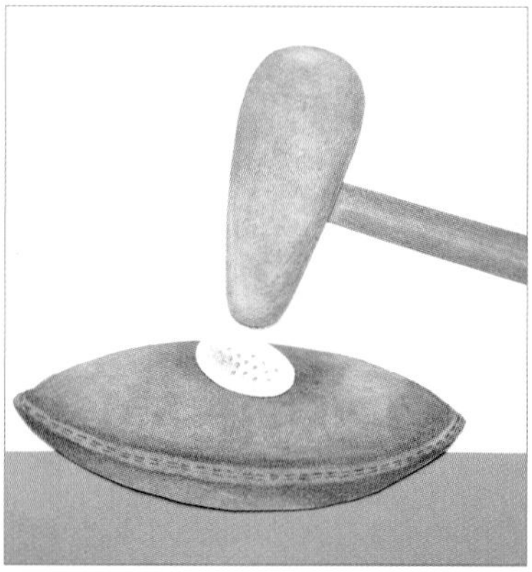

STEP 5 Put the disc in the sandbag and strike with a round-ended mallet to take the flatness out of the metal. This is just the first forming of the silver and will allow the disc to sit in the doming block more easily. Anneal, quench and clean.

STEP 6 Place the annealed silver in the largest hollow of the doming block, hold a large punch in contact with the disc and hit firmly with a flat mallet or hammer.

STEP 7 Continue to hammer from all angles. Move the round tool about so that the form is evenly curved; anneal if necessary.

STEP 8 File the edges of the silver hemisphere if uneven, or go straight to coarse emery on a flat block. Hold the dome firmly and rub it back and forth across the surface for a flat, even edge.

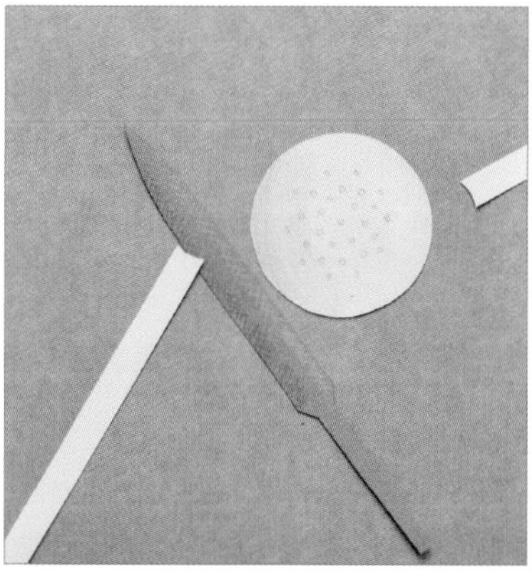

STEP 9 The bowl is now ready for the handles. Make these according to the design and file the handle ends to fit the curve of the bowl. Take time to get this line just right with a curved/ half round or ring file.

STEP 10 Set the work on the hearth so that all pieces are touching and cannot move whilst being heated. Flux the seam and paint the snippets or paillons of silver solder onto the joint.

STEP 11 Gently heat the silver so that the flux does not displace the pieces of solder. Once the borax has dried, turn up the heat and focus the flame so that both parts reach the right temperature together. Solder will melt and flow to the fluxed seam as soon as it is hot enough. Remove the heat as soon as the solder has melted.

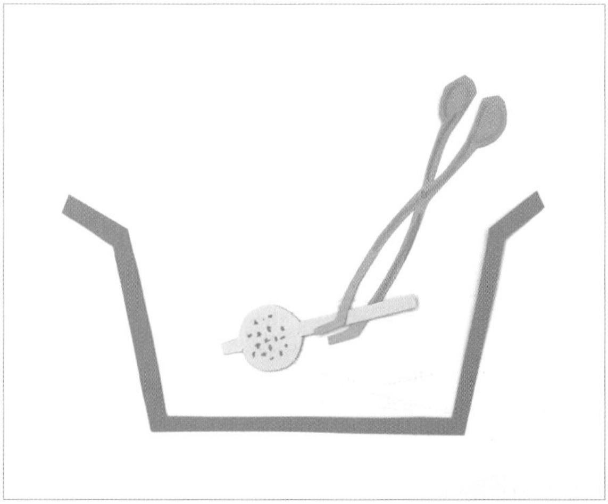

STEP 12 As soon as both seams are soldered remove from the heat and quench the tea strainer in water before placing it in the warm pickle to be thoroughly cleaned. Rinse in water after cleaning.

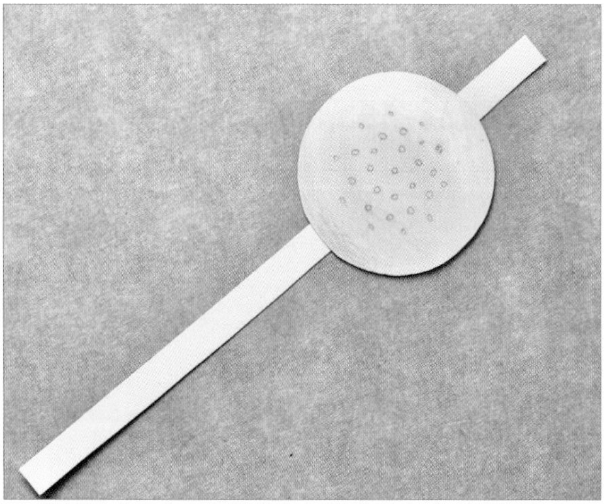

STEP 13 Tidy up the seams carefully with a needle file and follow this with emery paper in gradually finer grades to smooth the surface.

STEP 14 Polish thoroughly with Brasso and a soft cloth. Remove all traces of polish before celebrating with a cup of tea.

Creating the tea strainer without soldering

This is an alternative method in which the whole object is cut out from one piece of sheet silver. The handles are folded up before the piece is domed and then gently folded back into place after shaping. This design will sit slightly differently but works very well as a variation of the doming and drilling project, and because it is not soldered is a little quicker to complete.

This simplified version of the project does not involve any soldering so is a very easy approach to combining cutting, drilling and shaping.

Using two or more techniques to create an object starts to introduce new design and construction possibilities. In many cases this will mean confidence with the basics such as accurate sawing and filing so that parts match together properly, selecting the right hammer or mallet for the job to form metal and soldering neat and reliable seams.

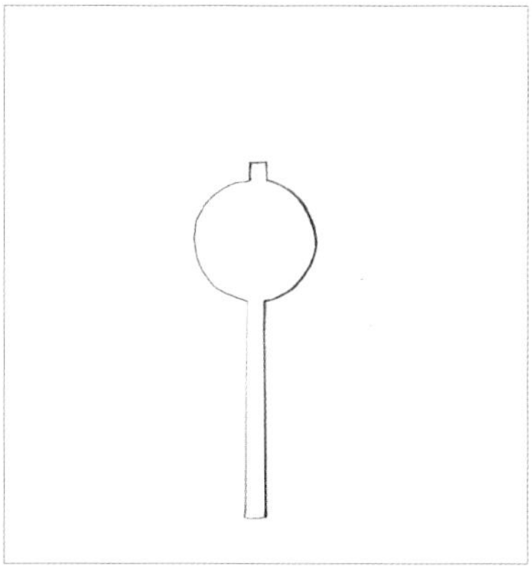

STEP 1 Draw the design to scale as a flat overview including the handles. Pierce out the sheet silver and file the edges. As before, the holes must be drilled before shaping.

STEP 2 Before doming the bowl of the tea strainer, gently fold the handles upwards so that it can be domed without the handle touching the edge of the doming block, as this will leave a mark.

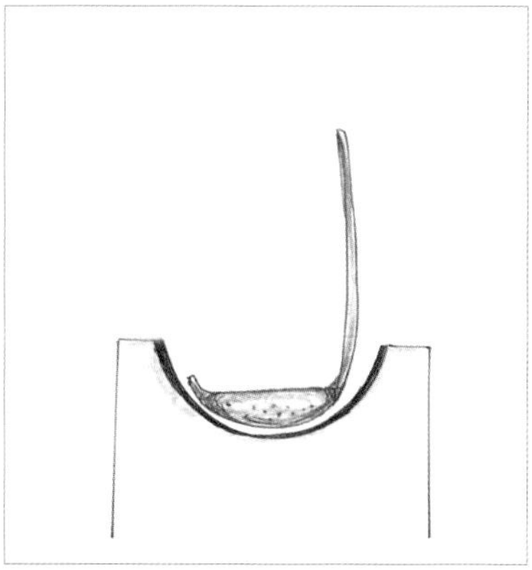

STEP 3 Shape the bowl in the doming block as before by tapping a punch with a mallet. Anneal and clean after shaping.

STEP 4 Press the handles back down into the correct alignment and mallet to shape on an appropriate stake or smooth surface.

CHAPTER 6

Forging

Forging is the process of hammering rod, heavy wire or thick sheet into a different form or cross section. Along with 'sinking' and 'raising' it is one of the principal methods of changing metal into a new shape purely by hammering. It is a skill that can be applied in a large variety of circumstances and is very satisfying to execute. This technique is used to create handles for vessels and spoons and can be used to create a whole object, such as a spoon beaten from one length of silver as in the example below. Spoons and forks are collectively known as 'flatware' and forging is the traditional silversmithing method used in their production.

Forging can be used to create a spoon from a single piece of silver.

Forging is an excellent way to produce sculptural flowing forms and decorative structural elements in larger pieces. The only limitation is that the heavier the gauge of the rod, the harder it will be to work. Repeatedly hammering thick metal can become tiring, but do not be tempted into thinking that a heavier hammer will speed things up. It will not necessarily be an advantage because tiredness will set in sooner and there is more likely to be a loss of control leading to annoying 'miss hits'. Instead, opt for a medium-weight hammer that can comfortably be used for as long as is needed. A heavier hammer can be tried once greater skill has been developed, along with a stronger hammering arm. The arm that does the hammering is not working on its own; the force needed to change metal is only as good as the hand that holds it steady on the stake or anvil. Sometimes the work cannot be held directly by the hand but will need to be gripped in tongs. This is because there can be some recoil when a solid chunk of metal is struck firmly by a hammer. Tongs will be much more comfortable on the fingers in such instances.

The principal tools for forging are a flat hammer, such as a basic flat-faced general purpose hammer of medium weight for basic flattening, a cross pein or vertical pein hammer for the initial forming stages, and a flat plate, anvil or stake to work on. With forging, the work must be supported on a solid surface and is generally in contact with this throughout the hammering process. In this way the material can be stretched and formed in a controlled, predictable manner. During forging there will be lots of repeated hammer blows while the metal is gradually being formed. It can be supported on an anvil, flat plate or stake fixed in the tree trunk or held in an engineering vice. Hammering is therefore the principal means of creating the object. There are dedicated spoon stakes for forming the bowl of the spoon and large doming punches can also be used for rounder shapes of spoon bowl. A planishing or smooth-faced hammer is used for final hardening and finishing.

As explained in Chapter 4, the amount of hammering will determine how often the silver needs to be annealed. Metal will only harden where it has been hammered so it makes sense to gradually work the whole piece and get as much done as possible between each anneal. When working on a big chunk of silver, remember it will harden just as much as a smaller piece of wire. Do not be tempted to overwork it because this will lead to cracking and metal fatigue. Keep the hearth as gloomy as possible so that the heat changes in the metal are easy to gauge.

Any object created by this technique can be left with the planished hammer finish or filed and polished to a sleek high shine. With just hammering it is possible to create a planished smooth bowl for a spoon. It does not have to be shaped by a file, but can be if wanted. In this case, a specialist curved file called a 'riffler' must be used and followed by whatever abrasives are needed to complete the curved bowl. This type of file is expensive but very useful for the bowl of a spoon or other similar shapes. Ideally the hollow part should fit over a stake, so that file work is not needed because the planishing has smoothed both the inside and outside.

For the project below I suggest using heavy wire of around 8mm diameter or a heavy rectangular section. If two spoons are being made it can be easier to start with a double length piece, which is worked from each end. This might be easier to hold and as there is one spoon at each end, the piece can be cut in two as the rod starts to lengthen.

DESIGN NOTES

A spoon comprises both a bowl and a handle so there is plenty of potential for design variety through the relationship of these two elements. Forging can be used to create a range of shapes at the end of the handle and it is possible to introduce a twist provided it is long enough. Hammering can be used decoratively by changing to a very fine cross pein hammer for linear patterns and textures. The bowl itself can be used to make a statement but if it is to be a large area, the size of the initial rod must be big enough to accommodate the spread without thinning the metal too much. This is why spoons such as ladles with a substantially larger bowl are usually made in two parts.

Health and safety

The work will be hammered onto a steel surface for this technique so remember to wear the ear defenders. To protect fingers from vibration, the rod can be held firmly in tongs or sturdy pliers. Cover the jaws with tape for a non-blemishing grip. Stout work gloves may not be essential but are a good idea for holding work during long hammering sessions.

Example 1

FORGING A SMALL SPOON FROM WIRE OR ROD

This first attempt at forging can be based on a design but without experience, it is very hard for a beginner to visualize how the form will develop. Start with a plan but be prepared to adapt it as the metal changes.

Tools

- Steel flat plate or large stake
- Raising hammer with forging face or heavy cross pein hammer
- Heavy flat hammer
- Ball pein hammer
- Planishing hammer
- Flat file and riffler file
- Emery sticks

Materials

Heavy gauge round, square or rectangular section wire, at least 6–8mm. The hammering will lengthen the material so the starting piece can be 30mm or about an inch less than the final design.

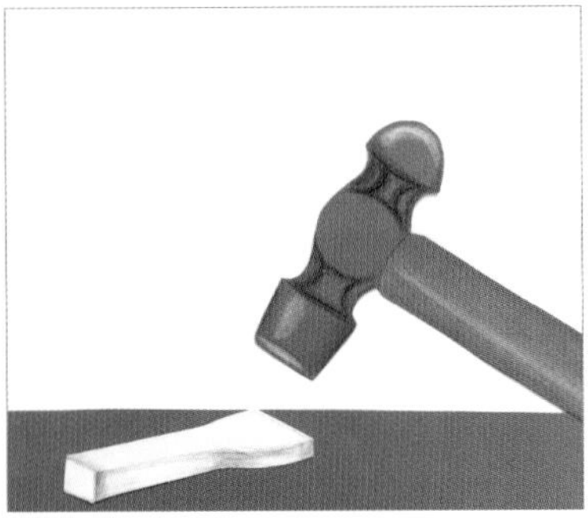

STEP 1 Start with the spoon end and using a heavy flat hammer on the flat plate, spread the silver to create an area the same length as the bowl part of the spoon. This flattened end will need to be annealed before further working with the forging hammer.

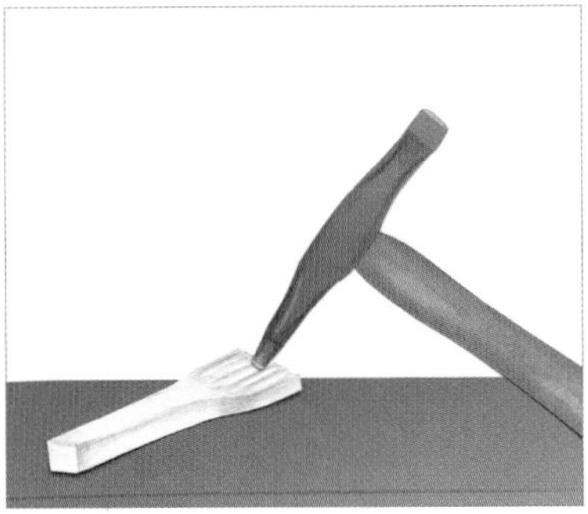

STEP 2 Use the forging hammer to spread the silver to the desired width of the spoon. A cross pein hammer will widen the bowl end when it is used in line with the handle. Anneal and repeat until wide enough, finishing with a flat hammer.

STEP 3 Use the hammer across the handle. This will spread the length of the handle. It can be hammered from the sides as well as front or back to alter the section.

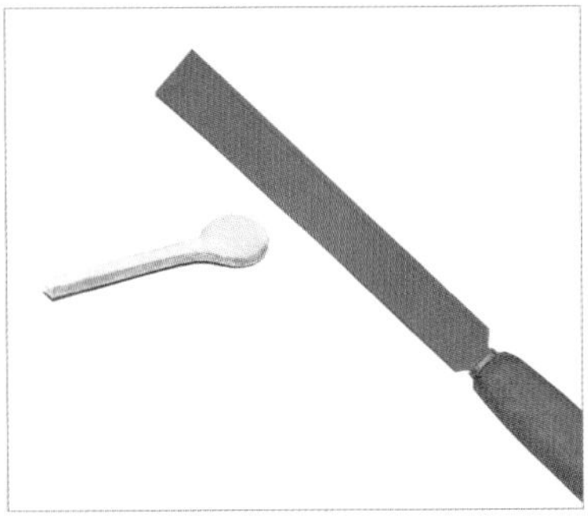

STEP 4 Draw the outline of the spoon bowl and cut to shape with a saw or large tinsnips, then file all the edges smooth.

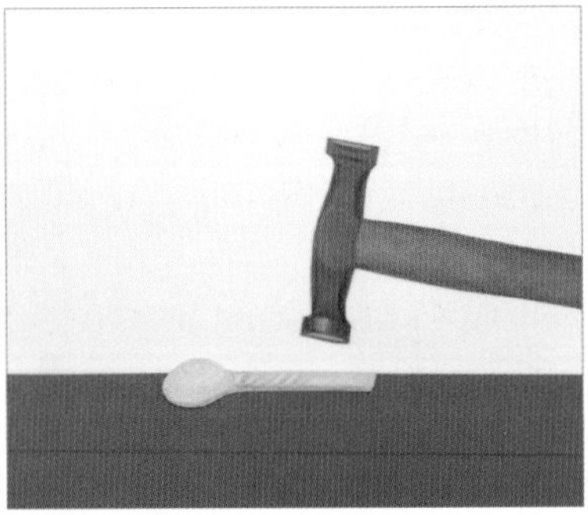

STEP 5 Smooth the forged handle by planishing on a flat plate or stake.

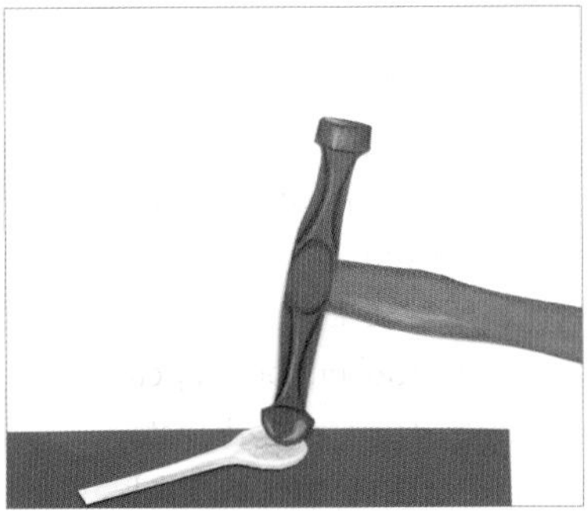

STEP 6 Form the bowl by sinking with the ball pein hammer. Take care not to hit the outer edge and stretch it. Anneal before further hammering.

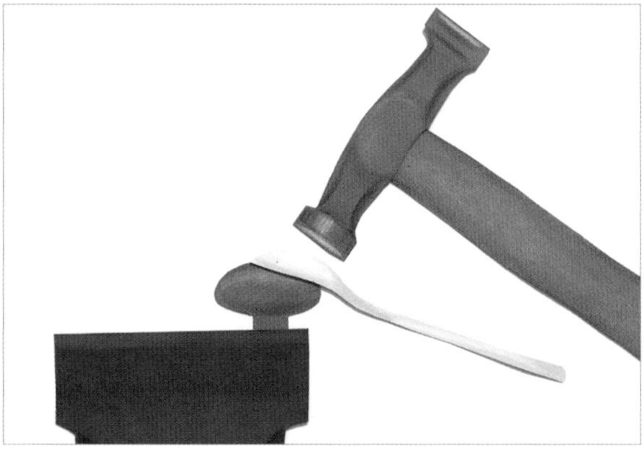

STEP 7 To refine the bowl of the spoon, place it over a special spoon stake or large doming punch supported in the bench vice and planish from the outside.

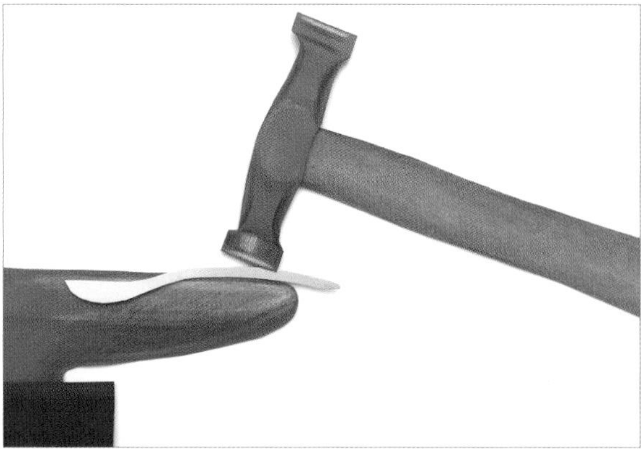

STEP 8 The handle can be planished one last time, taking care at the junction with the bowl of the spoon.

The spoon can be left with a carefully planished finish or it can be smoothed with the full range of abrasives to give it a sleeker finish. Emery sticks are very effective and relatively quick for working on the handle and exterior of the spoon bowl. The inner surface of the spoon bowl has been worked over a steel former during planishing, which will have left a smooth surface that needs no further work other than buffing with a soft cloth. If the stake or doming punch is blemished it is possible for this mark to be transferred to the surface of the spoon. For obvious reasons it is not possible to use an ordinary file on a concave surface, however if filing is absolutely necessary there are specialist curved riffler files that can be used. Riffler files are expensive to buy and there is no guarantee that one shape will suit all eventualities or forms. Having said, that a small selection of rifflers can be incredibly useful for working on unusual forms that for some reason cannot be finished by any other means. It may be possible to use motorized abrasives on a flexible shaft/pendant motor or dremel tool but be very careful when using these, as it is easy to damage work instead of enhancing it. Practice using small motorized tools on other surfaces first to get a feel for the amount of pressure needed and how to keep it under control.

Forging thick rod or wire is a versatile technique and is one of the principal methods of metal forming. Once mastered on a small scale, it can be tried out on a variety of projects beyond flatware. Below some of this methodology is applied to forming, but from thick sheet instead of wire.

Example 2

FORGING FROM THICK SHEET

It is possible to forge from thick silver sheet and in this example the project uses sheet silver at 3mm thick. There is less potential for the dramatic transformations that are achievable with heavy gauge rod but selectively thinning sheet can be a quicker way to create a small piece of flatware. This method cuts out the heavy work of hammering a chunky rod down to a thinner proportion but limits the thickness at any point to that which has been used at the outset.

Transfer the design directly onto the silver and pierce out the shape of the spoon. The piercing will probably be the hardest part of this project as 3mm thick is considerably heavier than is used for most projects. This cut-out shape is called a 'blank' and can be the same basic dimension as the finished spoon or slightly shorter if the blank is going to be lengthened and thinned. The bowl outline is cut out to the desired dimensions, as it will only be stretched in its depth through sinking. The bowl of most spoons does not need to be particularly deep, so it is more a matter of creating the right contours and curves that is important. Forging will thin and lengthen the heavy gauge of sheet and it should be worked until it matches the design profile at both the bowl end and handle end. As with the example above, remember to anneal the metal regularly as it work-hardens, and watch each hammer blow so that the shape is kept under control. Always finish the forming with some hammering so that the object is work-hardened enough to have resilience.

MAKE A SPOON FROM THICK SHEET

Tools list

- Steel flat plate
- Curved stake
- Spoon stake or large doming punch
- Forging hammer
- Planishing hammer
- Small hand files
- Emery sticks/polishing materials

Materials

- 3mm thick silver 120 x 25mm (approx)

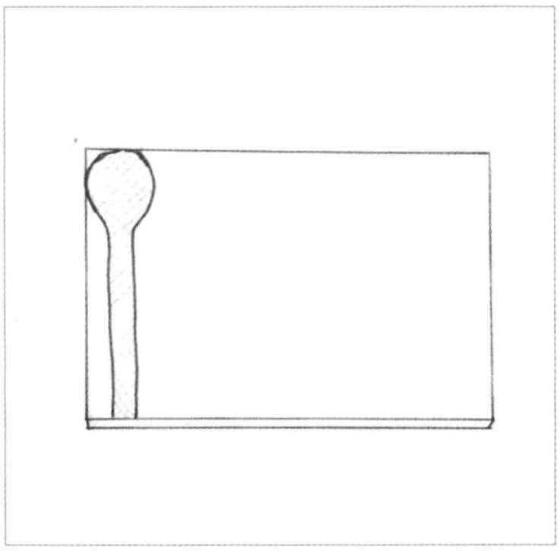

STEP 1 Transfer the design onto the silver and saw out the shape. Do not try to rush the piercing; this sheet is very thick so it will take time to cut it out neatly.

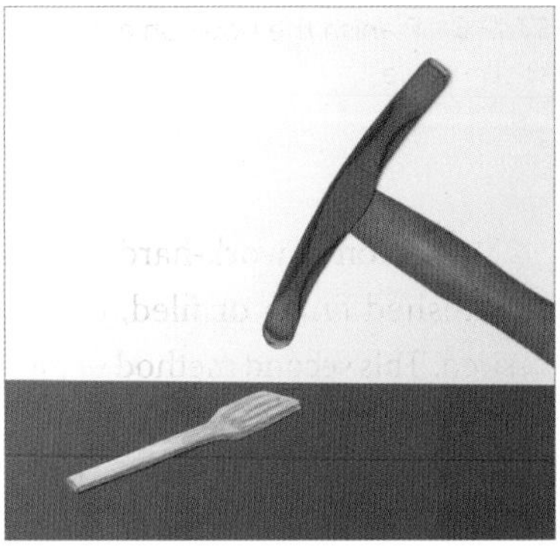

STEP 2 As explained above, the 3mm thickness is too thick for the bowl of the spoon but this will be reduced as it is hammered.

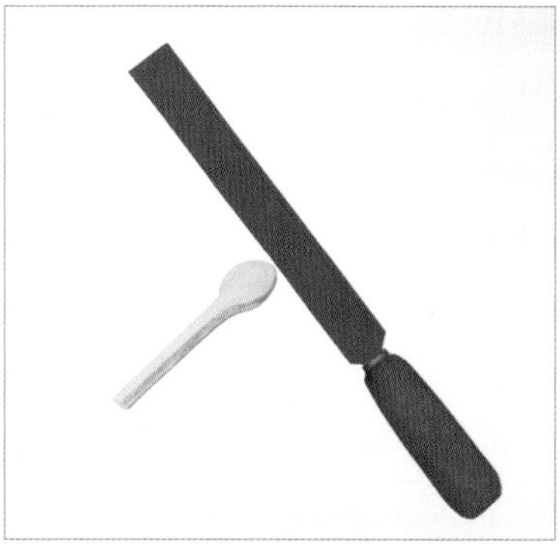

STEP 3 File the bowl profile into shape.

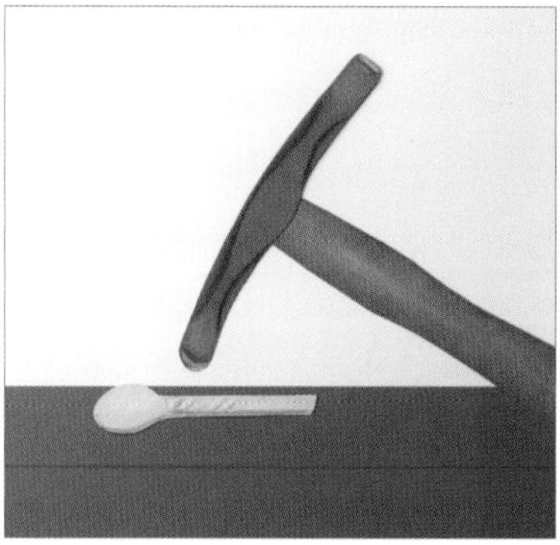

STEP 4 Forge the handle to the desired length and width. Anneal before further shaping and planishing.

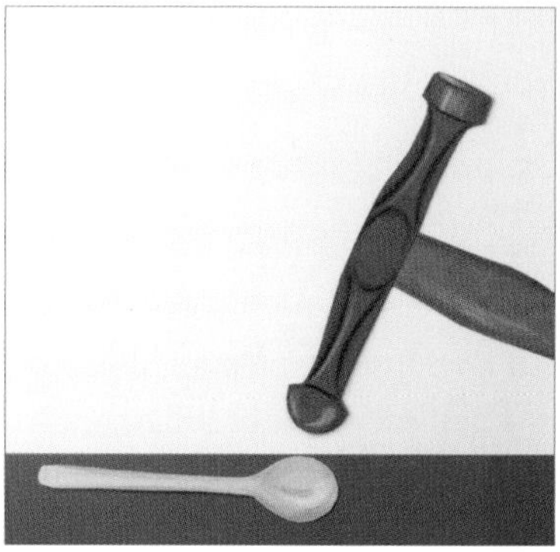

STEP 5 Sink the bowl of the spoon.

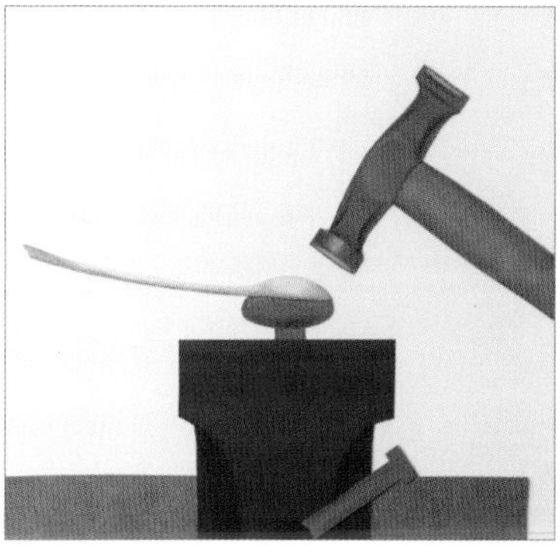

STEP 6 Planish the bowl on a spoon stake.

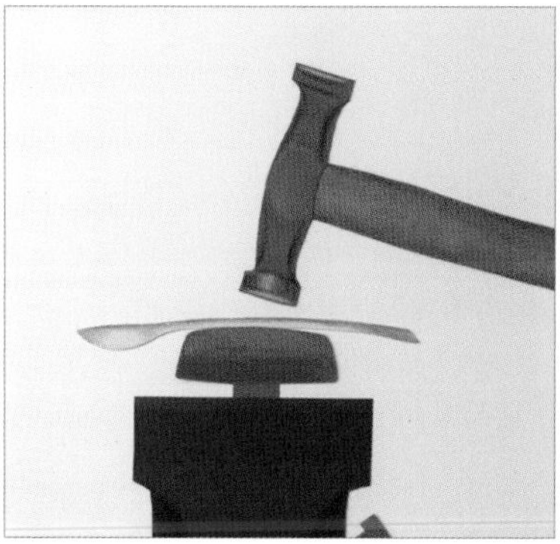

STEP 7 Planish the rest of the spoon to finish.

The spoon is work-hardened and can be left with a planished finish or filed, emeried and polished as desired. This second method of forming a spoon is fairly quick because the general shape is formed at the outset.

TAKING THE TECHNIQUE FURTHER

Working in heavy-gauge rod or thick sheet can be used to create other pieces to complement the spoon. An obvious complementary project is making a fork. A small cake fork or long-handled pickle fork can be made exactly as the steps above describe, using either thick square/rectangular rod or heavy sheet. The piece is formed as above, but with no concave bowl the fork end does not need to be hollowed but is instead left flat. The 'tines' or prongs of the fork are pierced out of the flattened end, which can be given a slight curve from the handle to create a well-balanced object to hold. Pickle forks should be long enough to reach into a jar and need only two prongs or tines sharp enough to skewer a pickle. Cake forks tend to be daintier, and about the same size as a teaspoon. A cake fork usually has three tines, one of which may be broader to hold more cake. The tines do not need to be long or sharply pointed but have a softer profile, providing just enough to hold a mouthful of cake.

FORGING FOR ORNAMENTAL FEATURES

Hammering a curved line

The forging face of the hammer will stretch the metal and this property can be exploited by just hammering selectively along one edge. As only one edge is being stretched, the whole piece will start to curve as the unworked side remains the same length.

Adding a twist to the handle

This is best done before the bowl of the spoon has been formed but the handle has already been shaped, filed and smoothed with emery paper. Anneal the handle ready for twisting and secure one end in the vice. (Protect the metal by putting on the vice guards first.) Hold the other end in strong pliers (again protect the grip area with masking tape or leather) and twist the silver round one or more times. After the twist is complete, the rest of the piece can be finished.

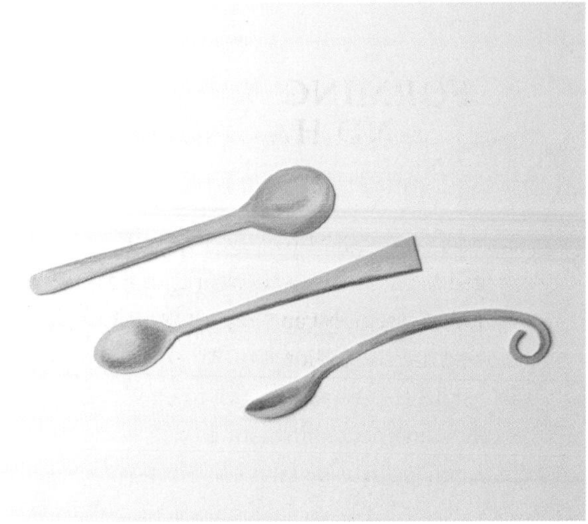

Forging and hammering can be used to create sculptural forms.

CHAPTER 7

Ladles and Spoons

FORMING A BOWL AND HANDLE

Spoons and ladles with a bowl too large to form from a single forged rod are made in two parts and then joined. This method of assembly can be applied to other objects created using these techniques of forming and these are adaptable skills for the silversmith to employ.

To make a deeper hollow suitable for a bowl, cup or ladle the metal can be formed in a wooden block. It may be possible to get a steel doming block which is large enough for a bowl of 60 or 70mm, but for a larger diameter it will be necessary to use a wooden doming block. Sometimes hollows can be carved directly into the tree trunk but if this isn't an option, it is worth looking for a commercially produced wooden former or finding a turner who can make something to order. A wooden block should be large enough to withstand plenty of hammering; there must be a border of solid wood around the hollow so that the overall form can withstand repeated mallet blows.

Ideally it is useful to have at least two hollow blocks with differing sizes so that a piece can be started off shallow before being pressed into a deeper form. To get the shape started and take the flatness out of the disc, do some very basic forming in the sandbag. Using a mallet will not harden the metal as much as a steel hammer

Spoons.

on a steel stake, but annealing is always advisable after this initial shaping so that the metal is easier to work at the next stage. The initial forming in the sandbag is also a good preparation for the disc of silver as it will help it sit in the first or shallowest hollow of the forming block. The curved and annealed piece is now ready for serious shaping.

The process of pressing sheet metal into a concave form is done in stages and is the same as using a smaller steel doming block. The metal is not being hammered against steel so it will not stretch as much as it would when sinking a hollow form. In this technique, the blank circle is being pushed into the wooden former with repeated malletting and as a result it will appear to decrease in width whilst at the same time becoming a deeper dome. To compensate for this slight reduction in diameter the blank disc can be cut out up to 10mm larger than the design.

To make a ladle, the large bowl shaped in the wooden doming block is one part of the project. It will also have a separate forged handle. These techniques have been explained in earlier chapters, but in this instance can be on a larger scale if desired. Making a larger piece will be more demanding of physical effort and concentration on accuracy. Likewise, the connection joining the bowl and handle will need to be a strong and inflexible junction tailored to the curves of both handle and bowl. This joint is reinforced by an extension from the handle that fits under the bowl. This is known as a 'rat tail' and is a tapered length of silver extending from the handle that is joined onto the exterior underside of the bowl. The join can be supported at the front with a similar detail if the bowl is cut out with a tab of metal to fit onto the handle on the inside.

The tricky part of this project is to join the two pieces together so that the handle is properly aligned and there is no gap between the bowl and the handle. It is very difficult to use binding wire to hold the two pieces together so this is usually done with split or cotter pins or titanium clips. The advantage of titanium is that it will not act as a 'heat sink' and draw heat from the immediate area making the soldering slower. The titanium is sold as a strip that must be formed into a useful shape to clip over the work, holding everything firmly in place while it is heated.

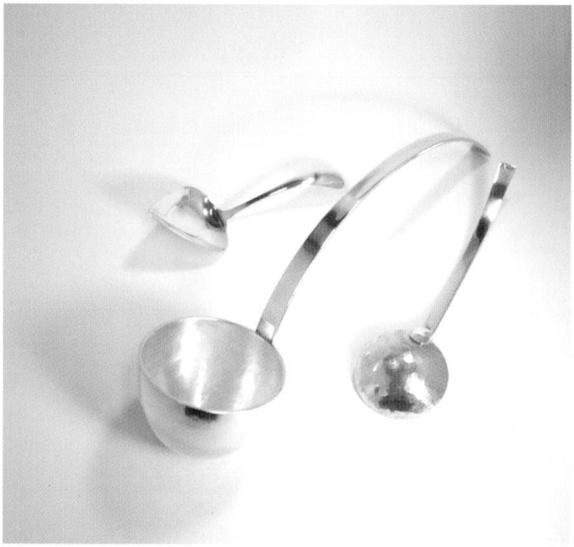

Spoons and ladles.

It is usual for larger objects to be joined with strip or stick-soldering rather than the method using small snippets. Strip soldering is perfect for larger objects that need more solder in the seam. With this method, a strip of solder is cleaned and cut about 2mm wide and 50mm long. It should be liberally covered in flux and held in reverse-action tweezers. It is held near to the work ready to touch to the seam when the correct heat is achieved. Being a larger piece it should flow throughout the fluxed area to be joined. After the soldering is done the piece can be cleaned up and finished, as no further hammering should be needed.

This brief explanation covers the basics of how a ladle or serving spoon can be constructed from two parts and the steps below illustrate this further. Before starting to do any of the making it is really important to spend some time thinking about the design potential for this project. A ladle can be for soup, punch or cream and a serving spoon has similar potential as a one-off object. As such, spoons and ladles lend themselves to being statement pieces, regardless of size and scale.

Obviously there is a function to distribute scoops of something delicious, but apart from this a spoon can be a special object in its own right when not in use. A long handle can be used to very dramatic effect by simple forging or twisting to create beautiful flowing lines.

At the opposite end of the scale there are very elaborate tea caddy spoons, which have small but beautifully decorated handles. Looking at traditional ladles and serving spoons may help with background research, and there are many contemporary designers making stunning one-off pieces. Remember that when finalizing a design it is never acceptable to copy another person's work. Instead use the research as an inspirational starting point for developing something personal, unique and of course achievable. This project is therefore an opportunity to expand in both skill and size by working on a larger one-off piece if desired or even developing a set or pair of serving spoons. Before embarking on the project, read through the steps below and do plenty of sketches to help visualize the potential proportions and feel of the piece.

The suggested soldering for a larger piece is 'stick feeding' the solder. This is a silversmithing method where solder is only introduced at the point of melting. It is not applied to the object beforehand in the form of paillons or snippets, but cut to a length of 50mm and held in reverse-action tweezers ready to introduce to the seam when it is hot enough. This technique can be daunting at first but placing a single paillon on the seam can indicate when the correct heat has been achieved. If wobbling hands threaten the accuracy of directing the strip or stick of solder to the right place, then build an arm rest of fire bricks as a support. The seam can also be joined with paillons, though this is easier where the contact area is smaller.

MAKE A SILVER LADLE OR SERVING SPOON

Tools

- A round-ended mallet
- A flat heavy mallet
- Sandbag
- Ball pein hammer
- Raising/forging hammer
- Planishing hammer
- Flat plate/anvil
- Doming block with a hollow large enough for a ladle

Materials

(Adjust as necessary according to the design of the ladle)

- 1mm–1.2mm thick sheet for a disc of 60–100mm diameter
- Thick rectangular, square or round rod (6mm or larger depending on the design)

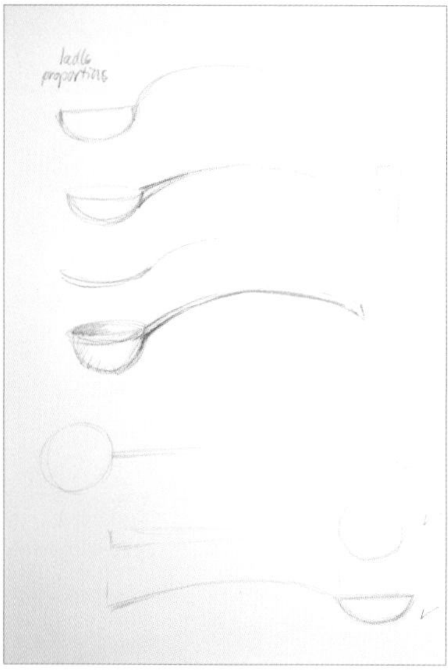

STEP 1 Draw the design as a 'plan' view, (looking down on it) and a side or 'profile' view. Draw to scale including the dimensions so that the two parts of the ladle can be compared with the design as work progresses.

STEP 2 Cut out the bowl blank and begin to form it in a leather sandbag with a round-ended wooden mallet. Try to keep the shape regular while malletting into a concave. Anneal and repeat.

STEP 3 Place the annealed slightly curved disc in the largest hollow of the doming block or wooden former and continue to work with the round-ended wooden mallet. Keep working over the same area to press the silver fully into the concave shape. Anneal and pickle before continuing.

STEP 4 After shaping in a concave former, the bowl can be refined by planishing it on a mushroom or domed stake. If there is an appropriately shaped stake, it can also be made deeper. Continue to shape and anneal as needed.

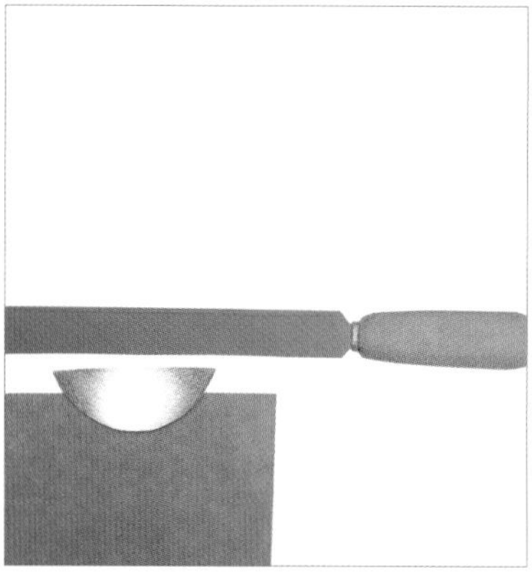

STEP 5 Check the shape and file the top edge of the bowl level.

STEP 6 Work on a steel flat plate to forge the handle to the desired shape and length with the cross pein hammer. Anneal as needed before planishing.

STEP 7 The rat tail of the handle will need to be formed into a slightly thinner flattened length to fit the underside of the bowl. It is meant to provide added support for the bowl but can also be a design feature.

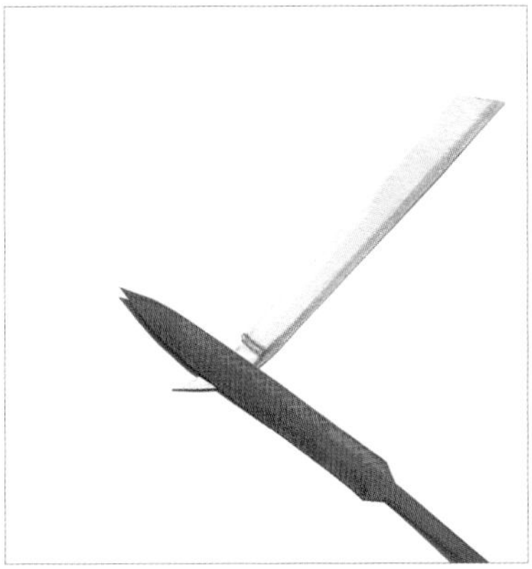

STEP 8 File away a small step inside the rat tail so that the handle will meet the inside of the bowl. Check that the curve still matches the bowl and reshape if necessary so that the two parts join in a smooth, continuous line.

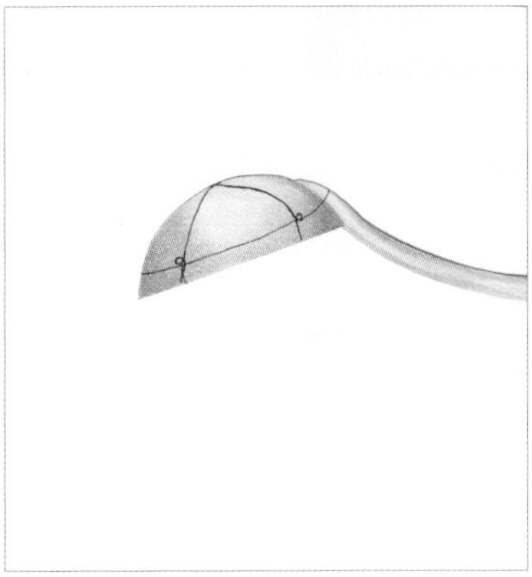

STEP 9 It may be possible to hold the two parts together with binding wire but the awkward shapes may be better suited to holding with split pins or titanium clips. Either way the setting up will take longer than the actual soldering.

STEP 10 When set up on the hearth, flux the seam thoroughly. Stick-feed the solder into the prepared seam once both parts are hot enough for the solder to melt and flow into the seam. Use binding wire or cotter pins to hold the parts together while soldering.

STEP 11 After soldering, clean in the pickle and check the seam to see if any area needs to be resoldered. When satisfied with the seam, the ladle can be filed as needed.

STEP 12 Check and adjust the handle on a stake, just using the mallet. Any distortion of the bowl can also be very gently tapped with a mallet but avoid working the area with the rat tail as this may leave an impression on the interior of the bowl, which is harder to clean up.

POTENTIAL ISSUES

It is worth pointing out that the construction may only be half of the story. Finishing a slightly larger piece may take longer than the previous projects. For a shiny finish it is essential to work through the grades of emery paper before buffing with a soft cloth and polishing compound. Regardless of the scale chosen for this project, joining two complex shapes together can pose problems. This is due to the combination of size and shape, in particular setting up awkward shapes for soldering. A longer handle can be difficult to balance on the hearth and may need to be supported with fire bricks so that it does not move once the heating begins.

Another difficulty is making sure that the bowl and handle are in contact and properly aligned. Remember that the handle can be adjusted after joining, so do not worry if the curvature is not perfect at this stage. It can be soldered and then reshaped to produce the correct curve. However if the handle is soldered on squint, this can only be fixed by removing it and starting again. In a worst case scenario the two parts have to be separated and carefully cleaned of all solder before being reattached. Reheating and separating the bowl from the handle, whilst theoretically possible, is difficult and could cause further damage. Instead saw the two pieces apart and take care not to compromise the bowl during this operation. This will probably mean that the rat tail end of the handle has to be sacrificed and any residue totally filed off the bowl. Although this sounds like drastic action, it need not be a disaster to the project. The handle can still be used; it will just be a little shorter once the end has been reshaped for a new rat tail. The remaining length can be adjusted without too much loss of character to the final piece.

Sometimes projects do not go to plan and whilst taking time and care should mitigate against disasters, it is also good to know that many can be remedied. As always, setting up properly in the first place is the answer but there will be times when the best laid plans can go awry. If something is not soldered on properly first time, do not despair. Take some time out and review what went wrong before tackling it again. Usually it is not a total disaster but a minor setback. Annoyingly, it is the mistakes from which much can be learnt.

Variations

The project above is based on a round ladle, but of course the bowl does not have to have this shape. Many serving spoons are formed over a dedicated spoon stake that is oval or egg shaped. Spoon stakes of different sizes are worth the investment if the plan is to make lots of them. A variation on this theme is to use neither the round doming block nor a traditional spoon stake. Instead the bowl is formed by sinking, as described in the very first project. This approach allows a different or unusual shape to be created such as the example shown where the bowl is a triangular form. It is the same principle in that the two parts are produced separately and then joined together with a rat tail for decorative reinforcement. Making a spoon is very satisfying and they can be interpreted in many ways and differing scales, so this is a project that can be endlessly revisited. A beautifully wrought spoon makes a unique present which can be used and enjoyed for years to come.

CHAPTER 8

Soldering Seams

MAKE A ROUND/PILL BOX

In this chapter, soldering is explored in greater depth. The use of heat to create a near invisible join allows silver to be transformed into three-dimensional objects with tops and bases, lids and spouts. This is not possible with just hammer forming techniques alone. It is the ability to add on other elements which make construction and soldering techniques an essential skill to master. So far the only soldered elements have been at one stage, such as joining a handle. Of course, many objects are constructed in such a way that there will be several seams or joins in a piece. Metal can be cut, curved or kept flat and then joined together with solder.

Silver solder is designed to be used to join silver because it closely matches in both colour and strength. It is mostly silver but with alloyed elements to lower the melting point, so that it is molten when the surrounding metal is not. There are different grades of solder with 'hard' being used for the first join and 'easy' being reserved for the final join. With a complex piece it is possible to have several seams with more than one being hard soldered and subsequent seams being medium then easy soldered. This allows objects to be made out of cut and formed pieces rather than stretching the metal over a stake. Making a constructed object can be quicker than making a purely hammered form and also allows the object to incorporate several elements. Parts formed independently can be joined to create a new form that would not be possible by hammering alone. For this reason, soldering is one of the essential skills to master because it opens the door to a huge range of possibilities.

Joining fairly small areas and short lengths together is not too difficult, but longer seams become more demanding. In theory it is not so different from small solder joins as there is nothing particularly complex about the soldering itself, rather it is the preparation of the seam. The longer the seam, the greater the need for careful measuring, accurate cutting and well-considered filing. Taking time and care at the preparation stage is important because silver soldering works by capillary action and the molten solder is a fluid which will flow

A round box with a hammered texture.

into the seam. Silver solder works best when the parts to be joined are a very close fit. All types of silver soldering rely on this principle of close-fitting parts into which the solder is drawn when molten. A well-soldered seam will mean there is a strong connection between the attached parts and it will be almost invisible when finished.

The prepared edges must be clean, and fully in contact wherever they are to be soldered. If the metal is annealed it will be soft and unlikely to spring apart when heated. This may not always be relevant but is worth considering if there is any risk of distortion or tension in the structure. Due to the nature of many projects, it is likely that the elements to be joined will have to be held in place whilst the heating takes place. It is advisable to make sure that the work is sitting on the fire bricks in a secure position and the parts are held together firmly with clips or binding wire. The heat source must be able to reach all parts to be joined without overexposure of delicate areas or small details. Flux is always essential for the solder to run into the seams but if binding wire is being used, take great care to avoid getting flux and therefore solder on it. If this happens it must be filed off before going into the acid. Binding wire is made from iron and it would permanently contaminate the cleaning acid, which would then have to be disposed of. It would also turn silver pink due to the plating effect caused by iron in the acid.

The project to create a cylindrical box with a push-fit lid is a good place to extend skill and confidence with different soldered seams. These steps can also apply to a non-cylindrical-shaped box.

Design is important in this project because the proportions will determine the level of complexity. For a first attempt at making a round box, avoid making a design that is very tall in relation to its diameter because the longer seam means there is a greater length of tightly curved metal to control. Instead design a box where the height is no more than one and a half times the width. This is a bit more manageable for a first try because the curvature of the body of the box is less pronounced in relation to its depth. The estimation of the overall height should include the depth of the lid. The whole box, lid and body are made as one length of tube and then cut into two parts after soldering. Sawing these apart is quite difficult to do but it ensures that both lid and body are exactly the same.

The rod of steel that is used for forming the cylinder will be the guide for the box before and during production. Basic maths can be useful in making correct measurements but is not essential in this project – indeed the exact dimensions are not particularly useful because the metal need only be a loose fit on this former. Instead use some graph paper and wrap it loosely around the rod. This will show what the finished box will look like and it is easy to adjust the proportions at this stage before committing to metal.

Make a loose-fitting model of at least 5mm wider than needed to wrap around the forming tool. This will ensure that the tube for the body of the box will have a loose fit on the steel form and can be turned round on it with ease. If the model is made to fit the tool exactly it is unlikely that the metal version will ever fit round the steel rod, because the metal sheet is much thicker than a paper pattern. The extra millimetres of allowance on the pattern includes a couple of millimetres for the thickness of the metal, and any that is lost when the edges are sawn out and filed true. Use the model to work out the height of the finished box, which includes the push-fit lid. Making simple models from paper will help refine the proportions of the box before the rectangle of sheet silver is cut out. The other parts for the base and lid can be cut after the first stage is complete.

Once the size is decided it must be cut out accurately. Use an engineer's square and mark out the 90-degree angles at each end. Pierce in a straight line and remember that any wobbles can be filed before the silver is formed into a tube.

Bullion dealers sell silver sheet cut to order so it might seem like a good idea to request a piece of the exact size required. Generally this can be very useful for some projects, but unfortunately it is not an advantage in this instance. When silver is cut for sale it will be cut by a guillotine, which has a shearing action that slightly compresses and curves the very edge of the metal and it may not be absolutely millimetre perfect. In addition to this main piece there will be two other parts needed for the base and the top so work out a size of sheet metal that will accommodate those three elements in the best layout possible. When planning the shopping list there will also be an inner sleeve or bezel that can be made from a thinner gauge of sheet. It is worth having some thinner gauge sheet for small details or non load-bearing parts of projects such as this. The instructions below show the steps in making a plain box, although it can be decorated with a hammered surface, which is very effective when polished. *This is included as an option at step 10.

ROUND BOX WITH PUSH-FIT LID

Tools (picture)

- A round steel rod
- A large rawhide, wooden or rubber mallet
- Small cross pein hammer for surface decoration (optional)
- Steel rule, dividers and scriber for marking and measuring
- Flat plate and engineer's square for keeping the work true
- Depth gauge
- Piercing saw, back saw
- Hand file
- Iron binding wire
- Pliers
- Emery paper and flat emery sticks

Materials (picture)

- 0.8–1mm sheet depending on box size. Allow enough to cut out the surrounding wall, top and base.
- 0.6 or 0.7mm sheet for the internal bezel. This will be a strip long enough to fit inside the box and be between 7–10mm deep.
- Hard silver solder

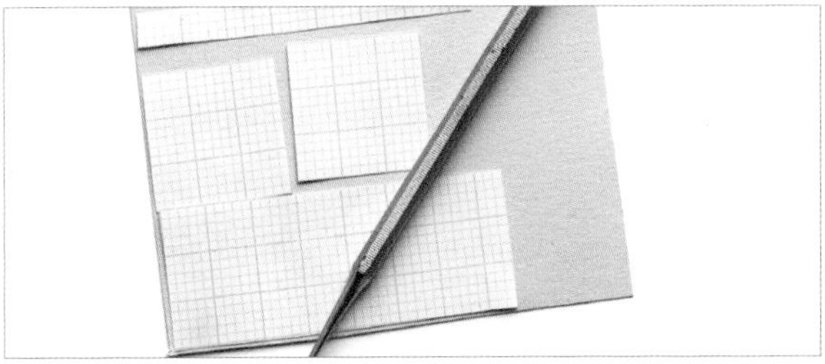

STEP 1 Prepare the layout on the silver with a paper pattern. Design the box and draw it from the side and top, marking down all measurements. Think about the best layout for all the parts before cutting out.

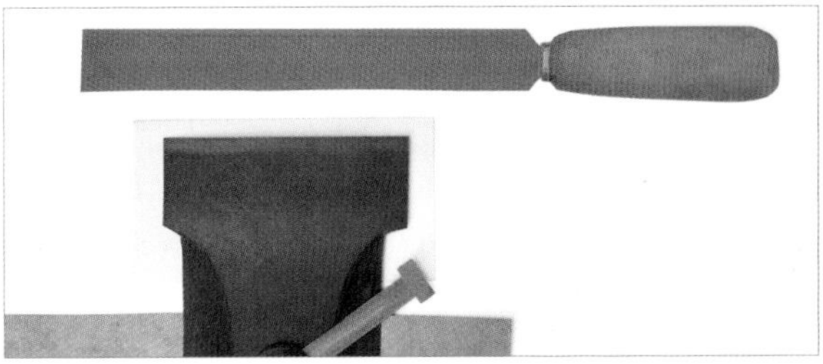

STEP 2 Cut out the rectangle with a piercing saw, taking care to keep the cutting straight. Use vice guards and secure the silver sheet in the vice low down, leaving only a few millimetres of metal visible so it doesn't bend when filed. File all edges true.

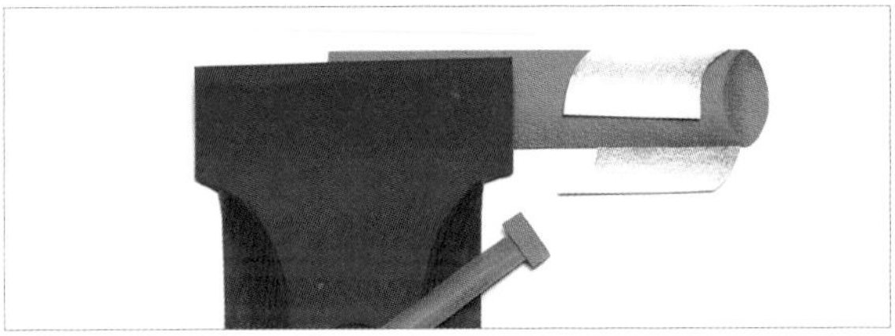

STEP 3 Remove the vice guards and put the rod or forming tool into the vice. Hold the sheet metal firmly against the rod and press the sheet around it by hand.

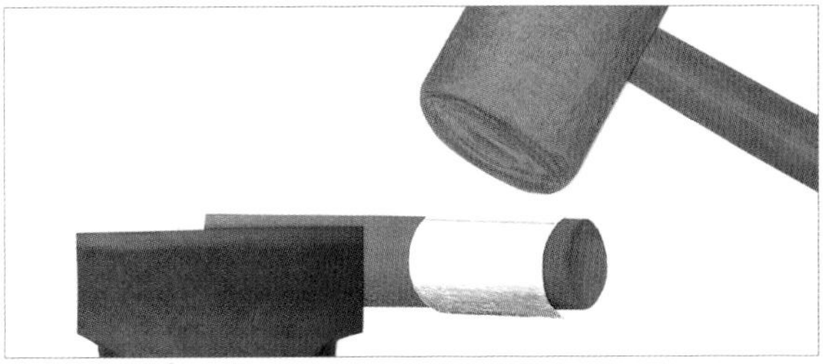

STEP 4 Close the seam with evenly distributed mallet blows. If the silver is resistant, anneal and clean it before checking the seam one last time.

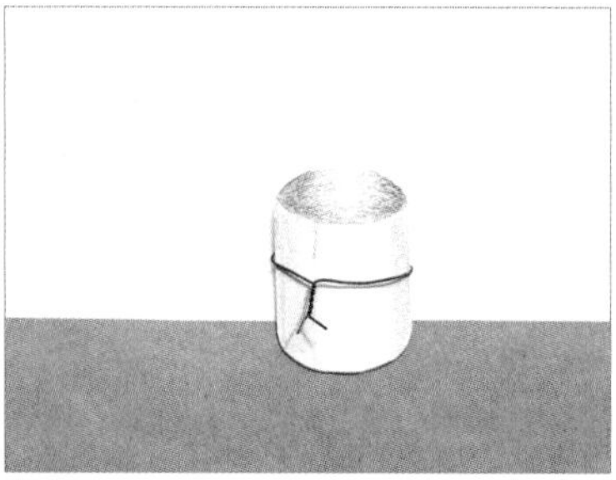

STEP 5 Align the seam and secure it with one or two binding wires. Tie the wire exactly over the seam and tighten with a kink to one side. This allows for expansion so that the wire does not cut into the silver surface.

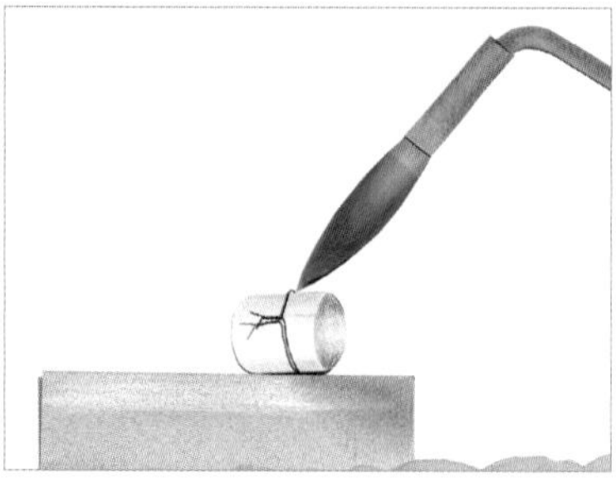

STEP 6 The clean, bright edges are essential for soldering. Flux the edges from the inside and out and apply firestain protection if desired. Make sure the cylinder is in a secure position on the hearth and cannot roll while it is heated.

STEP 7 For beginners it will help if a snippet of solder is placed at one end of the seam to indicate when the melting point is reached, then when the temperature is high enough introduce the stick of solder to fully seal the seam.

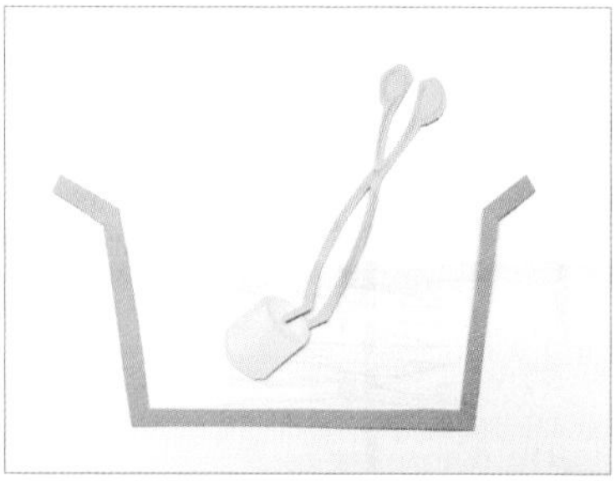

STEP 8 Quench the work and remove all traces of iron binding wire and file off if necessary. Place in the pickle to clean, then rinse and dry. Always check that the binding wire is removed before pickling.

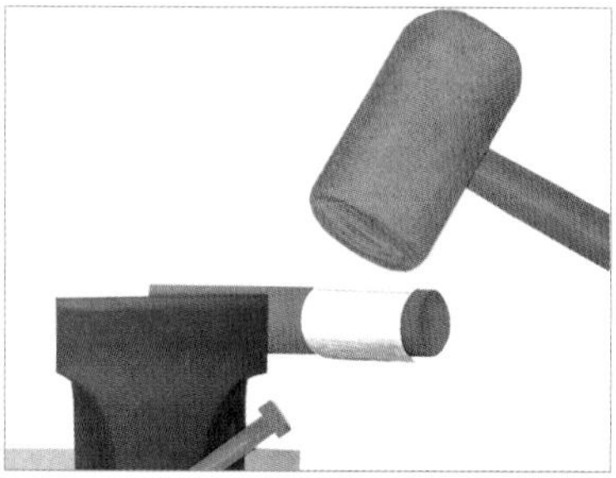

STEP 9 Shape the tube on the steel rod with the mallet. Perfecting the circular shape must be done now because once the ends are soldered in place, the form will be fixed.

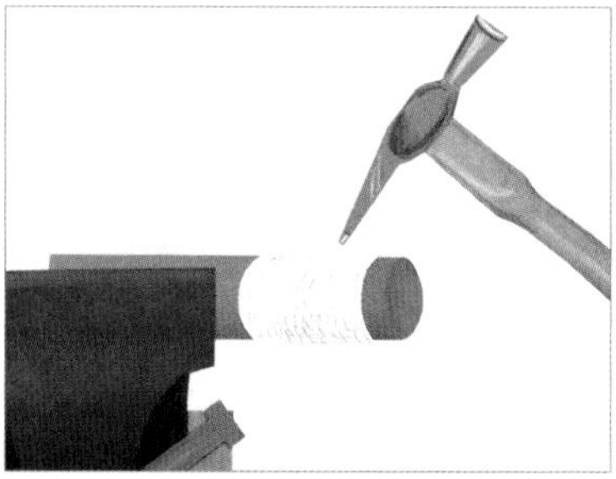

STEP 10* A hammered pattern cannot be added later. It is optional, but this is the time to add a texture or pattern to the surface before continuing to the next stage. Focus on keeping the hammer marks evenly distributed.

STEP 11 Tidy the seam and file off any excess solder. Check that the top and bottom edges are absolutely level by emerying back and forth on a flat plate.

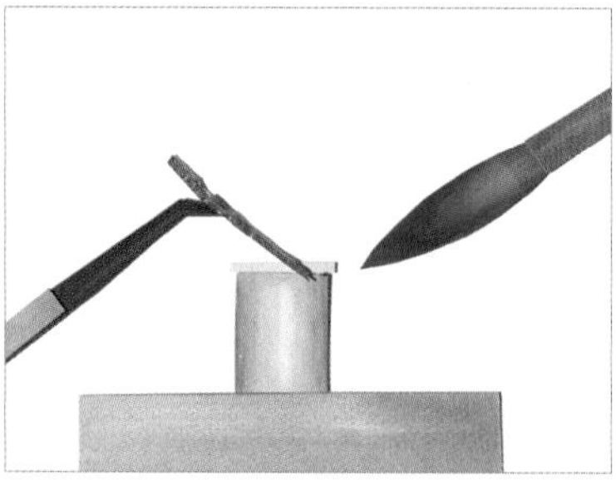

STEP 12 Cut a disc for the base 1mm wider than the box. It can be soldered on upside down with the base sitting on top or from below if there is a wire mesh to support it. Either way is acceptable for soldering and binding wire can be used to keep it in place.

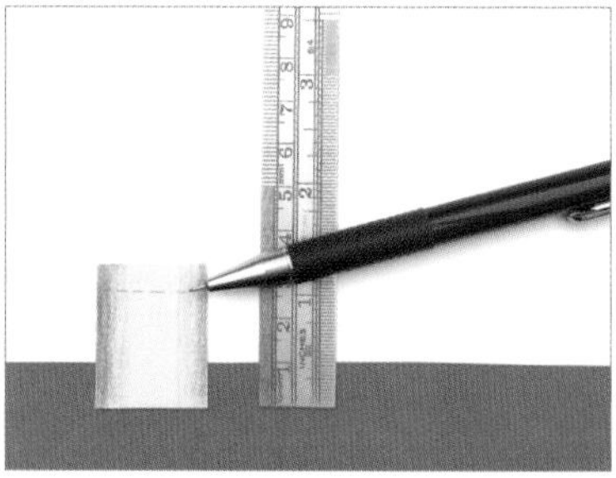

STEP 13 Check the box is still round by easing it onto the former, then place it on the flat plate and measure the line of the lid. Mark it all the way round. Cut out the lid and pattern if desired at this stage.

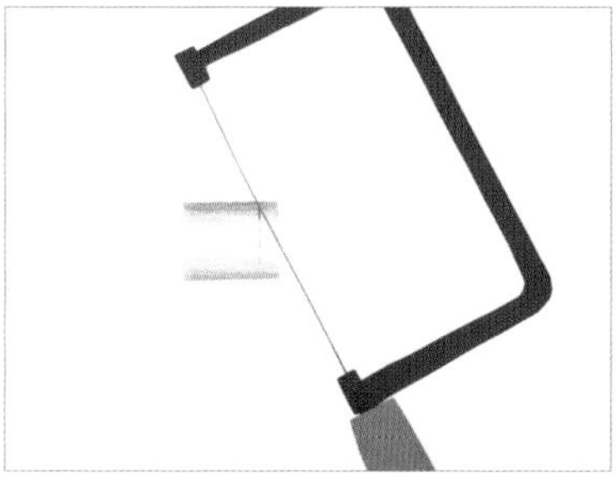

STEP 14 Before soldering on the top of the box make a small saw cut into the line at one point. This will allow hot air to escape during soldering. Never solder a fully sealed hollow object.

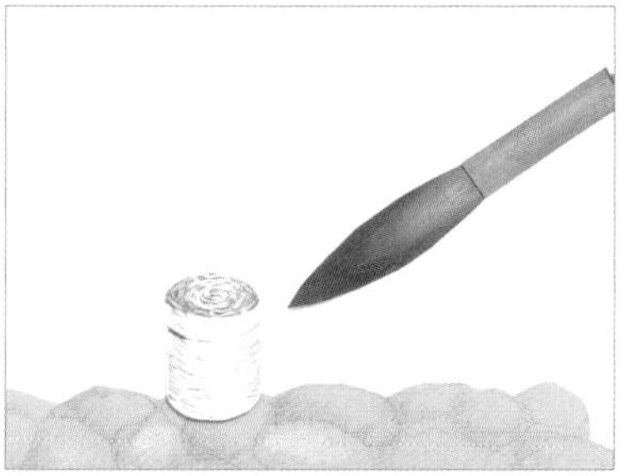

STEP 15 Solder the prepared top onto the box. Binding wire can be used to hold it in place. Do not quench or pickle, but cool it under running water after soldering.

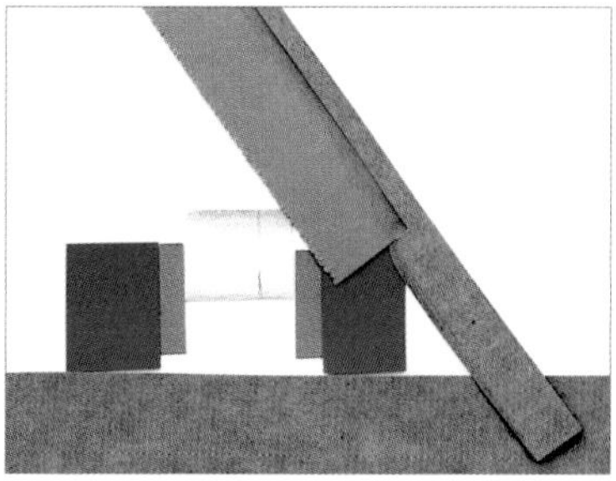

STEP 16 Take the cooled box and cut it apart. Either hold the box carefully by hand, or loosely in the vice to cut apart with a back saw. Only a flat-topped box can be held in the vice; if it is domed it must be hand held.

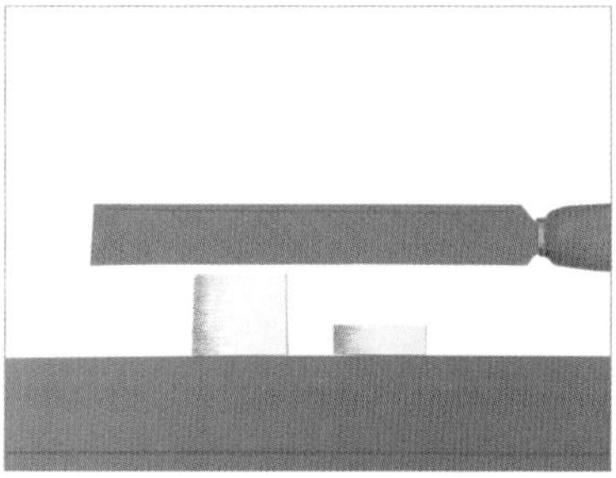

STEP 17 Clean both the lid and box. Both parts must be filed absolutely level and flat so they match perfectly when put back together. A round box should have a universal fit.

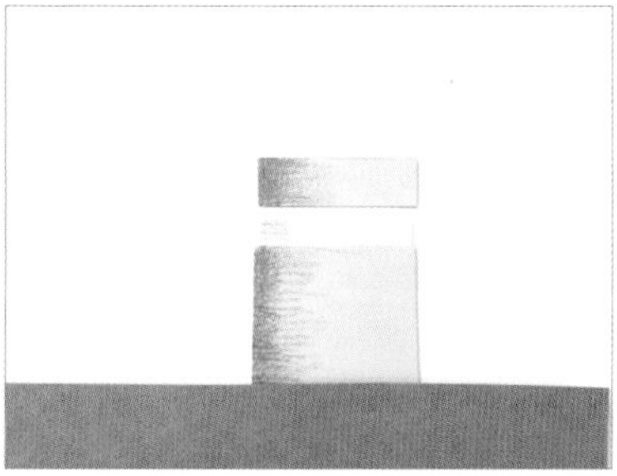

STEP 18 The lid of the box will fit onto an internal sleeve soldered into the box. This sleeve or bezel is 10mm deep x the internal circumference of the box. Make an accurate template then cut the strip from silver. Solder into a circle.

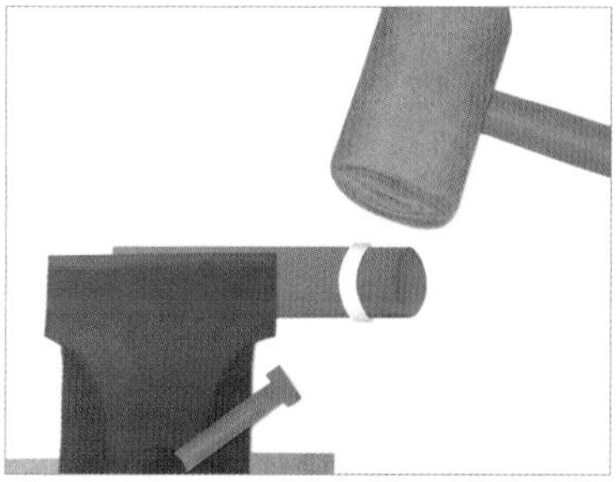

STEP 19 Cut and solder the bezel together. Mallet the bezel round and check it is a firm fit in the box. If it is too tight, file it to fit. If too loose, tap with a hammer to stretch it a small amount.

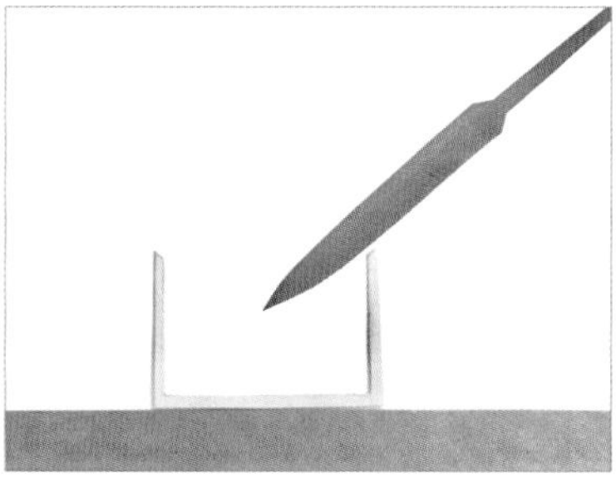

STEP 20 File the inner edge of the box wall at a slight inwards angle. This will provide a channel for the solder so that it does not impede the proper fit of the lid.

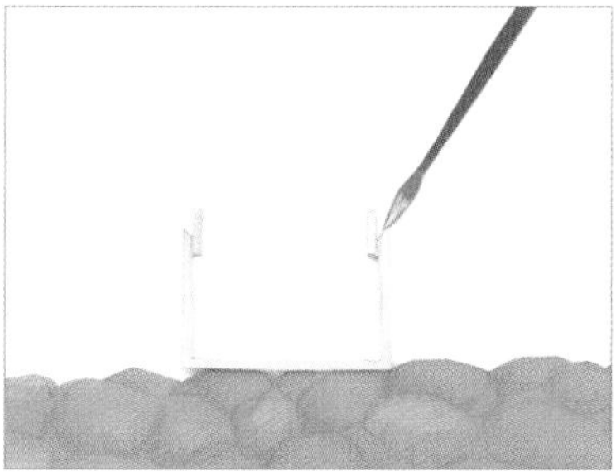

STEP 21 Push the sleeve into place with 5mm projecting above the height of the edge, and flux the seam. Use paillons or snippets of easy solder placed at regular intervals for this join or try stick feeding again.

STEP 22 The box and lid are both finished. Some tidying up may be needed so check that the lid fits properly, adjust as necessary and polish the two parts together.

Finishing

All of the steps in making the box have now been completed and all that remains is to finish the outside. If it has been given a decorative hammered surface it will need little more that a quick rub over with very fine emery paper and then a buff with a soft cloth and Brasso or other polish. For a sheer finish on the surface, use different grades of emery stick for a sleek shine all over. At this point the lid should fit, but if it is too tight the bezel can be carefully filed or emeried just a smidgen. If the lid is too loose, lie the box on its side and burnish the bezel from the inside, pressing down to ease it out a fraction. The interior of the box can be finished in various ways.

Satin finish

This can be achieved quite quickly with a piece of rubber grit such as Garyflex block or powdered pumice on a wad of damp cotton wool. Rub the chosen abrasive around the inside surface to create a neat directional finish.

Oxidizing

Silver will gradually blacken and tarnish over time. This natural discolouration can be accelerated and controlled by using a sulphurous compound to instantly blacken the surface. There are several oxidizing solutions commercially available, such as Platinol, which work very well on prepared surfaces. Make sure the area is clean and free of grease to ensure even coverage. Being sulphur based it is rather smelly to do, so make sure there is good ventilation or apply the liquid outdoors. Rinse away the excess, dry and seal the blackened area with a little restoration wax.

Gold leaf

Gold leaf is an extremely thin tissue-like sheet of pure gold that is applied directly to a prepared surface. The adhesive used is a lacquer or varnish that has a setting time which allows for preparation of the leaf to be cut to size. It will stick onto the touch-dry varnish to form a rich layer of gold. It can take a bit of practice to perfect the application of gold leaf because it must not be touched with anything other than fine tweezers or a clean paintbrush. When completed it has a beautiful colour and can be burnished to a rich, lustrous surface once it has fully dried. Gold leaf is different to gilding, which is a chemical process where particles of gold are electrochemically deposited and bonded onto the surface of silver. Some smiths have the equipment to do this themselves but usually work is sent to a plater to be gilded or plated. Gilding is used a lot for the interior of drinking vessels to add a luxurious glow to the concave surface.

Leather, textile or fine paper lining

Thin 'glove weight' leather can be used to line the box. There are various adhesives that can be used with it. It is best to cut the leather with a sharp craft knife and fix it so that it fits neatly below the bezel.

The same technique can be used for textiles or beautiful paper to line a box interior. Always use glue with great care as any excess can spoil an otherwise beautifully made object.

The cylindrical box project has a great many steps but taken individually non are particularly difficult as long as enough time and care is taken with measuring and filing accurately. In fact, once these stages have been mastered it is a very versatile method of construction and can be adapted to make special objects in a variety of shapes and sizes. The box can be ornamented with details such as working a hammered finish onto the body, as detailed at step 10. Alternatively the cylindrical body of the box can be left plain with just the lid decorated. The top can be slightly domed, textured or patterned, all of which creates added detail. The same methodology can be applied to making a box in another shape as long as there is suitable tooling for forming the body. Remember the lid will not have a universal fit if the box is oval, for instance.

CHAPTER 9

Making a Hinge

Many silver objects have a lid or top that is an integral part of the piece.

Instead of the two parts being totally separate, such as a box with a push-fit lid, the container or vessel has an attached lid that is joined at the hinge. This means that the top and base are designed and constructed from the outset to include a hinge. This sounds rather obvious but it is stated because there are a few points in the construction of the piece that will specifically relate to this mechanism.

A standard hinge is suitable for most containers with at least one flat side but can also be used on round or curved objects, such as a pill box or salt cellar. In those cases the hinge will need to stick out beyond the curved wall or be supported on a bearer plate to create a flat edge on the otherwise round item. Creating a hinge requires more patience than just making a top to go on something, as it is a mechanism that must work reliably and fit perfectly.

KNUCKLES

A hinge allows two parts to be joined but to move independently so that a lid or door can open whilst still being attached to the rest of the object. It is made with little sections of tube that have a central pin to allow for rotation or opening. The hinge pieces are arranged with the greater number of sections on the base of a box. Each section of the hinge is called a 'knuckle', and it is usual for a hinge to be made up from an odd number of knuckles. A longer 'piano'-type hinge takes great skill to construct so a large box with a long side might have five knuckles on the body of the box and four between these attached to the lid, making a total of nine knuckles. To keep things simple for this first attempt at hinge-making the example will only be a total of three knuckles; two on the base and one on the top.

Box with hinged lid.

The knuckles are made from tube or 'chenier'. (This French word may have come into usage due to the influx of skilled silversmiths amongst the Huguenot refugees who settled in London's Spitalfields.) A small tool for holding the tube while it is cut to size is called a chenier vice and it is well worth getting one for this project, as it can be used on many other occasions. It holds the tube steady so that the ends can be cut and filed absolutely flat at a 90-degree angle. The hinge relies on the parts having accurate right angles when cut into pieces. No hinge will work properly if each carefully measured section is not square or 90 degrees at each end.

A thick-walled chenier is frequently used for hinges because although this part of an object is small, it needs to be strong. Not only must the ends be at right angles but there must be no tiny lumps or burrs of stray metal, which could impede the smooth rotating action of the hinge when finally put together. Unfortunately there is nowhere to hide if there are errors, so each step along the way has to be correct for the end result to work properly.

As well as using a cutting guide for those square ends there usually has to be a straight parallel groove into which the knuckles will sit in an absolutely straight line. For this it is worth making a scraping tool to use as a file for the final shaping. Metal would normally be scraped away with a file, but files are tapered which means that any groove would also be slightly flared and therefore not truly parallel. The filed/scraped groove must also be a good fit for the tube, which is going to sit in it. Using a much smaller tool will stop the chenier sitting properly and a larger groove would have too much room to move, which is exactly what is not wanted for the knuckles to stay in line.

Parallel files are available but can be expensive and may not be the right size for every project. Sometimes a riffler or curved file is useable, but again these are expensive and may not be totally parallel. A scraper made from steel rod or an old file can be tailored to have the same diameter as the external measurement of the chenier. An alternative is to customize a cheap file that is the right size for the project. Break off the tapered final third or half of a round file so that the remaining piece is now straight along its reduced length. This tool is only suitable for a hinge that is fairly short in length, such as the box project below.

The individual knuckles are soldered to just one part, either the top or the base in an alternating arrangement. Obviously the knuckles are not joined to both parts, otherwise the hinge will not be able to rotate in the carefully prepared groove, but this could happen by accident unless great care is taken when soldering. There are various methods for making sure that the solder only flows exactly where it is wanted. It is possible to inhibit the solder at very specific points by applying a paste of rouge and water or alternatively use a lead pencil to draw over the area being protected. If rouge paste is being used it must be applied sparingly and allowed to dry before the flux and solder is put in position. In general a pencilled line is easier to do because of this. Flux should also be applied sparingly in this project with the solder cut into small paillons for accurate positioning. It is important to buy thick-walled tube/chenier for this project but a description of how to make tube from scratch is included at the end of the chapter. It is a handy skill to have or know about just out of curiosity and to add to your general knowledge of techniques.

There are various different types of hinge and the description below is a step-by-step guide to doing a basic hinge for a flat-sided box. The chapter includes a description of making tube, although this is not essential to the main project as tube is a product that is readily available in lots of different sizes.

The body of the object needs to be constructed first and the lid designed and made so that the two can to be joined at the hinge. These skills share many similarities with jewellery making and goldsmithing because the majority of this work will be done at the bench. It is inevitably more fiddly than some of the hammering projects where there are frequently only one or two parts to the finished object. Working on a small scale does not make something easier or quicker to produce, indeed it can often mean the opposite. Making a good box requires patience, accuracy and time so in order to make a hinge, it will also be necessary to make the item that will be fitted with this mechanism.

Health and safety

There are no problematic issues with the above projects but it is important to be aware of maintaining good deportment for comfort and concentration. Much of the time will be spent sitting at the workbench, so as a matter of good practice make sure that the seat is in a low position in relation to the bench with no need to stoop over the work surface. The working area should be well lit with a magnifier to hand if needed. Do not stay in the same position for hours on end but take time out to stretch arms outwards to the side, upwards and behind the back. This will relieve any build-up of tension in the shoulders. To counteract the clenching action of keeping the fingers tightly gripped, relax the hands with a good shake and then splay the fingers apart and gently press onto a flat surface. Try to make time for a quick break outside to look into the distance in daylight, which will give the eyes a rest and a change after close work.

This project requires more close work than some of the others in this book and it is strongly recommended that all reading or close work spectacle prescriptions are kept up to date to avoid unnecessary eye strain. Always allow plenty of time and avoid the unnecessary stress of setting a deadline for a new technique, which is quite demanding of concentration due to the accuracy needed at each stage.

Example 1

MAKE A HINGED BOX USING READY-MADE NAPKIN RING SECTION

The first project below is devoted to making a box from a ready-made section of napkin ring tube. This is a fairly quick method of making an interestingly shaped pill box which will have a hinged lid. Various shapes are available from bullion dealers and the piece selected for this demonstration is octagonal, measuring 43mm across × 25mm deep. The other shapes available are an elongated oval with round ends, an oval with two flat ends or a 'D'-shaped section with a curved front and flat back. As the selected shape is fairly shallow it will not be cut in two as with the round box, but will have a flat lid to which part of the hinge is soldered. This product is sold already formed therefore it is more expensive than regular sheet or wire. However, the advantage of using a ready-made product outweighs the added fashioning cost, keeping the focus on making the hinge itself.

The first stage will be to prepare a simple wooden former to fit the selected shape. To do this, any type of offcut wood will do. The silver was drawn around directly onto the end of the square length of wood and it was filed down making sure that each facet was absolutely true. The octagonal section is fairly straight-forward to shape as it more or less means taking the corners off and adjusting it until the fancy tube can fit firmly, but not so tight that it can't be removed. Anneal both the tube section and the base before soldering them together. This will remove any stress within the sheet and minimize the potential for distortion. The base sheet does not need to be particularly heavy, so 0.8mm is adequate although it can be made to match the wall thickness of the napkin ring at 1mm. The inside of the hinged edge will have an additional support to provide extra metal for the tube. The lid will be made of a slightly thicker sheet which has a hammered pattern, made with a special texturing hammer and the extra thickness will provide a better contact for the section of hinge.

For those who do not want to use this ready-made section for the box, this chapter also includes a description of an alternative method of making a flat-sided box but with rounded corners. The method has been kept fairly simple so that making the hinge remains the main focus of the projects in this chapter.

Tools

- Filed-to-shape wooden former
- Selected large and needle files
- Steel flat plate
- Texturing hammer
- Wooden mallet
- Chenier vice
- Titanium clip or reverse-action tweezers
- Coarse, medium and fine emery papers

Materials

- Section of ready-made napkin ring tube, annealed
- Sheet for base, cut to shape and annealed
- Support strip for the hinge
- Heavy sheet for the lid
- Thick wall tube
- Wire for the hinge

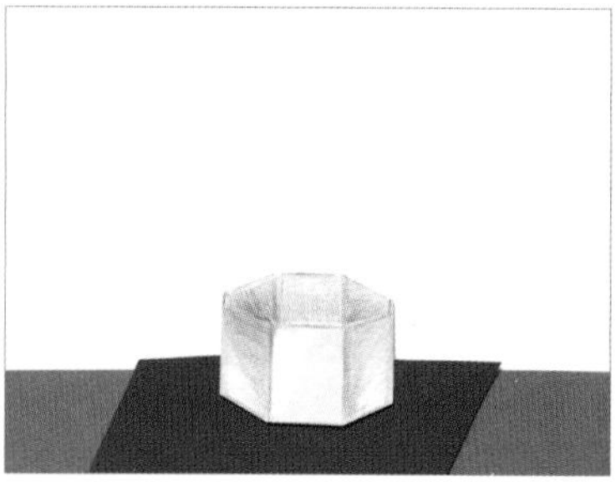

STEP 1 Check the base edge is flat by rubbing it on medium emery paper on the flat plate.

STEP 2 Hold the box and base together while soldering. To avoid distorting the flat sides, just hook the binding wire over the walls to keep the base in place rather than tying all the way round.

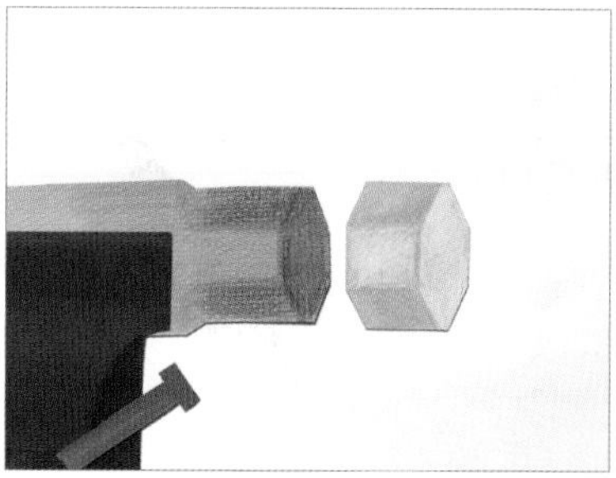

STEP 3 After soldering, check the shape is still true by carefully pushing onto the former. Do not use a mallet as this could damage the flat sides.

STEP 4 Measure and cut to size a support strip to solder just inside the top edge where the hinge will be located. Hold it in place with a cotter pin. It is probably easier to use paillons when soldering this small seam.

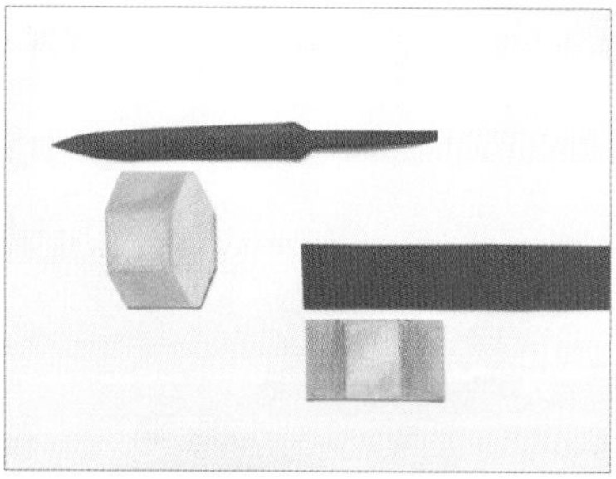

STEP 5 After cleaning in pickle, file the base flush with the walls and neaten the top edge with medium then fine emery sticks.

STEP 6 Prepare the lid of the box. Cut it to shape and decorate as desired.

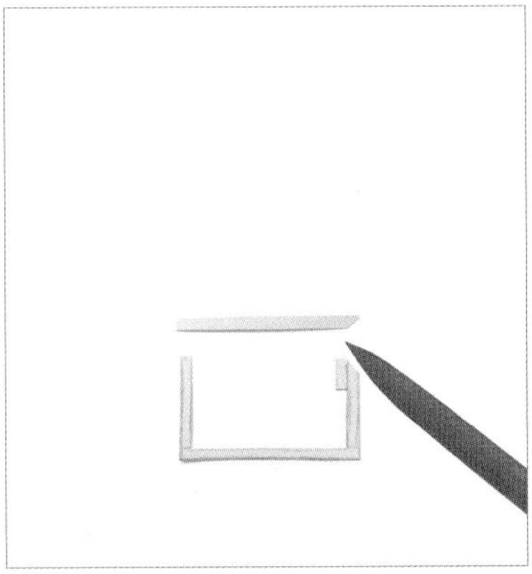

STEP 7 File the reinforced top edge of the box at an angle. Then file the lid edge to a matching angle.

STEP 8 The angled edges create a 'v' shape, which must be rounded to accommodate the hinge tube. Scrape or file into a curved groove for the hinge.

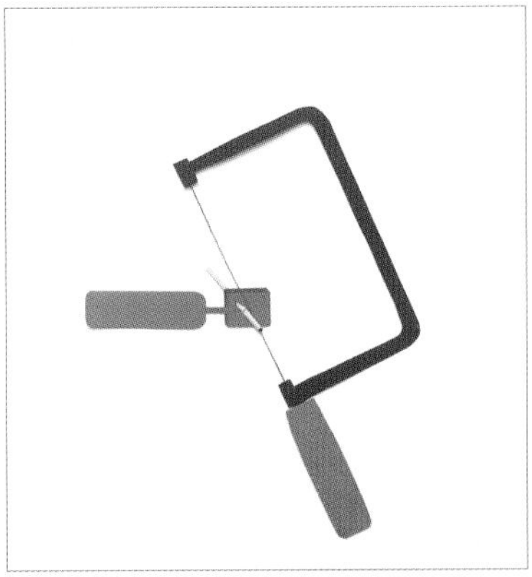

STEP 9 Measure and mark the hinge then cut the tube into three lengths using the chenier vice and a saw.

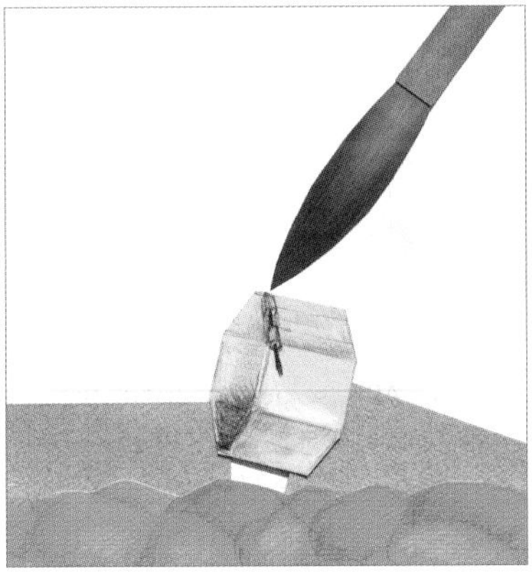

STEP 10 Paint rouge and water onto a steel wire or a thick sewing needle and let this dry before feeding two pieces of tube onto it. Carefully position the wire in the prepared groove. Use small paillons to avoid excess solder.

STEP 11 Check the exact position of the knuckle before soldering it onto the lid. After it has been soldered, the box and top should fit together again.

STEP 12 Taper a slightly too tight wire very gradually along its length. Poke the wire into the assembled hinge and pull it until it is very firmly wedged in. Cut off the excess and very carefully file it flush with the angled hinge.

The box is now complete in terms of metalwork. The interior can be lined with another material, oxidized or gilded to transform it into a little treasure.

Example 2

A SQUARE BOX WITH ROUNDED CORNERS

Tools
- Wooden former
- Chenier vice
- Engineer's square
- Steel ruler
- Piercing saw
- Selection of files
- Ball pein hammer
- Round scraper or straight round file to match the tube
- Straight steel wire or a sewing needle to hold the hinge during soldering

Materials
- Silver sheet for the wall, base and lid
- A length of thick-walled chenier/tube just longer than the hinge
- Wire for the hinge, usually steel or hard draw silver at an angle. When the lid and base are held together, this will appear to be a groove.

The four walls of this box are made from one single strip, which is formed into a square over a tailor-made former. This is very similar to making a round box so there will be just one side seam. To begin with, take a square section length of wood and file it to the required shape, creating softer corners but flat sides for a soft square.

This method of construction uses the same methodology as the round pill box in the previous chapter. It is based on a forming tool made by the smith to their own specifications rather than using a round steel rod. The wooden block is the template for the body of the box, which will have just one vertical seam with the addition of the base and top. The wood supplies just enough resistance to act as a basis for forming the body of the box but do not expect it to have the durability of a steel tool.

This method of making a box can be translated into a variety of shapes, although of course any lid that is hinged can only be attached to a straight edge. Any wood can be used, it just needs to be filed to shape; the example below was a leftover from some DIY which had been square in section. The centre line on one side was marked on the wood for the location of the seam. A simple paper template was wrapped around the former with an allowance of 2mm added for the thickness of the metal. As with the round box, the total depth includes 5–10mm for the lid. The wooden former allows the shape to be supported while a saw line is cut before a top is soldered on.

Before cutting out the silver for the surrounding wall, measure the wooden former and remember to add on 2–3mm. If the silver does not fit around the shape, the wood will have to be whittled a fraction!

Draw a centre line on one side. This will be at the back of the box.

STEP 1 File all of the edges true, taking particular care at the two ends that will form the side seam.

STEP 2 Wrap the silver around the wooden former starting from the centre line marked on one side. Press the silver carefully to take on the shape of the wooden former. Line up the centre back seam.

STEP 3 Bind and solder the seam with hard solder, quench and clean before shaping with a mallet on the former.

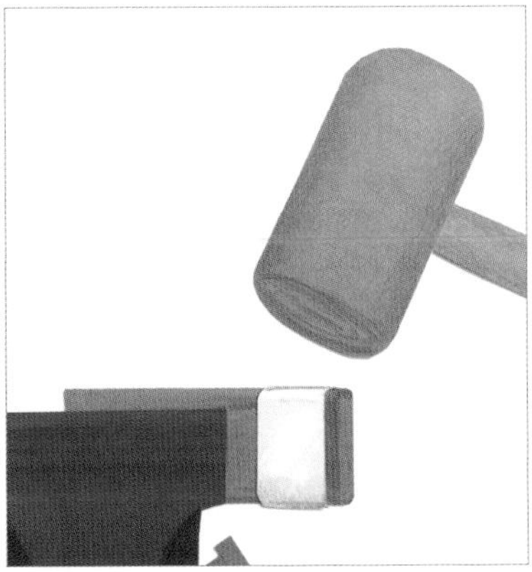

STEP 4 Mallet the shape true, making sure the seam is lined up with the centre mark on the wood. File the base edge flat and shape the top edge to a gentle chamfer to fit the slightly cushioned top.

STEP 5 Cut out the base sheet allowing a small margin all the way round and solder this onto the box. Binding wire can be used to keep it in place during soldering.

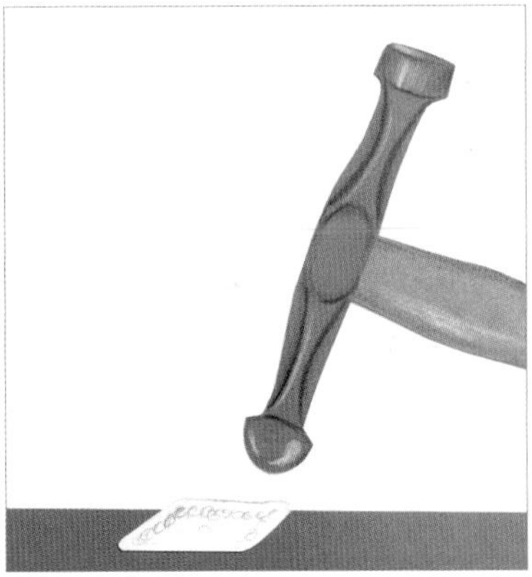

STEP 6 After cutting out, the top of this box has been shaped into a cushion form by sinking. Use a small ball pein hammer to sink the top sheet into a gentle curve. Check the formed top fits the box then anneal it.

STEP 7 Mark the line where the lid will be cut off. Place the box on the former for support and very carefully cut through each corner, leaving just the centre sides attached.

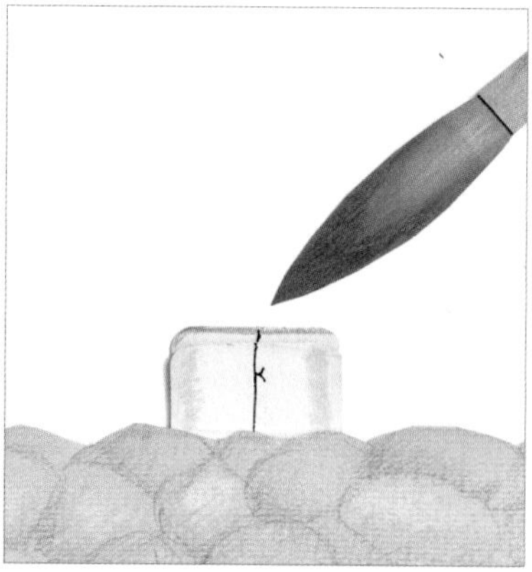

STEP 8 Tie the top onto the box with binding wire to keep it in place while it is soldered on. Do not quench or pickle, but cool the soldered box under the tap.

STEP 9 Hold the box and saw it apart from each corner. After separating the lid and base they can be cleaned in the acid.

The instructions from this point are the same as for the previous box.

- Both base and lid will need to have a reinforcing strip or wire soldered inside to support the hinge.
- Measure and cut each piece and solder these into the box and lid as shown before.
- File and emery the edges so that the box and lid meet in a closely fitting line.
- The hinge must sit in a groove. Angle the box edge and then file a matching angle on the lid section.
- Tape the box and lid together and shape the groove into a rounded trough for the tube.
- Measure the length of each section of tube; there should be an odd number; either three or five pieces.
- Cut the knuckles using the chenier vice as a guide. Keep the saw blade close to the side of the vice.
- Once cut, the pieces can be assembled on a rouged steel wire or needle.
- Rouge inhibits solder and should be used sparingly so it does not inadvertently stop the sections soldering to either the box or the lid. The wire will keep the knuckles aligned during soldering.
- Tie the box and lid together and set on the hearth with the hinge area uppermost.
- Place the supported hinge in the groove.
- Use minimal flux and place a paillon of solder next to each knuckle where it joins either the base or lid.
- Solder the hinge onto the box and lid, then quench.
- Remove the binding wire and steel needle before pickling the two parts.
- The separate parts can be topped up with solder if necessary but use the steel support wire to keep pieces aligned.

Hinges often have a steel wire but silver wire is acceptable for a small, short hinge. Start with a longer piece of wire which is slightly too tight to go through the tube. File or emery a very gradual taper along the wire. Feed the thinner end through the hinge and use pliers to pull it until it is firmly wedged in the tube. Trim off excess wire, leaving it a smidge longer at each end. If the tube is squared off, the wire can be spread by hammering it on a flat plate. If the tube is filed to follow the contour of the box it can be filed flush.

SALT CELLARS

Making a beautiful hinge is one of the more demanding projects in this book and once a basic hinge has been mastered, it is possible to start looking at different versions of this useful mechanism and the many ways in which it can be incorporated into other projects where a lid is called for. Round vessels such as a jug or decanter could have a hinged top and this next project does exactly that but on a smaller scale. Salt cellars or 'salts' can be an open little bowl, but are frequently a closed container with a lid and tiny spoon. The serving of salt in a special container at the dinner table has a long history, from the exquisite household relics of Pompeii to the outrageous opulence of the famous Benvenuto Cellini salt cellar. A more recent tradition for salt cellars is the glass liner which can be removed for cleaning. Salt cellars are particularly associated with the blue cobalt coloured glass from Bristol, which became fashionable for ornamental salt cellars from the late eighteenth century onwards. The blue glass liners are fairly easy to find online or in antique shops and due to their ubiquity are not very expensive. The rich colour of the royal blue glass is particularly attractive next to silver.

Before starting it will be necessary to find a blue salt liner and base the design to fit it. Choose one that is cylindrical in form so that a silver surround can be made into which it will fit. Some of these glass liners are very slightly flared but as this shaping is very slight, it is probably simpler to make a parallel cylinder form into which the glass will fit; just make sure that the outer sleeve of silver is based on the largest diameter of the glass. To make it easy to remove the glass from time to time, the base can either have a hole in it or a thick wire soldered inside.

To exploit the gorgeous colour combination, the salt cellar will be made from a sheet of silver which has a cut-out design to highlight the contrast of materials. The hinge on this object will be created in a very different way, which is fairly simple but effective for a small object. In this instance it is a good idea to make a paper pattern from the glass but as always, allow just a little extra length for the thickness of the metal.

The pierced-out design will have to be done before the side seam is soldered because sawing through a closed shape would be very difficult to control. Transfer the design to the blank sheet and mark all of the cells that are to be cut out. Avoid taking on anything that relies on strongly geometric patterns if measuring and sawing skills are not up to scratch yet and instead opt for something that cannot be spoilt by an occasional wobble. For those who love geometric patterns and crisp angles it is a good idea to draw the design onto graph paper, which is then stuck directly onto the silver with a glue stick. It is easy to see and saw through and means there is no risk of leaving any scribed lines directly on the surface of the silver. If doing a freehand design holds more appeal, it is easy to remove the plastic film from the surface of the silver and replace it with masking tape. The tape is a good surface to draw a design on and again is easy to cut through.

A small drill hole will have to be made for each cut-out compartment so that the saw blade can be fed in and tightened before cutting begins. Use a centre punch to tap a tiny dent before drilling to ensure there is no slippage of the drill bit. Any swarf or shreds of metal around the drill hole can be removed from the inside with coarse emery paper. The next stage is to feed a saw blade through the hole. Always start with one end of the blade firmly secured in the piercing saw and slide the silver sheet towards this closed end. Hold the saw in one hand while leaning the frame against the bench edge. This action will compress the frame while the blade is tightened with the other hand. Once the blade is firmly in place, the frame will relax outwards ensuring the blade is drawn tight along its length. Most saw blade breakages result from the blade not being as taut as possible, allowing too much movement and therefore the possibility of snagging and snapping.

There will be a lot of starting and stopping to retighten the saw frame but it is worth persevering because once mastered, piercing is a very effective way of creating a decoration. If the cut-out areas are very small they may be too tiny for a file, so really give the design some careful thought before starting and where possible use a fine saw blade such 0/4 or smaller 0/6. Another point to remember when planning the design is making sure that the cut-out pattern lines up when the seams are put together.

The external shape of this little salt pot has two small tabs at the top edge, which will become part of the hinge. This method for attaching a hinged lid differs from the earlier description and is another way of making two components work together in a flexible attachment. The two tabs are set at an angle leaning towards the seam, because when the form is shaped into a cylinder these will splay out, becoming parallel. Check the exact angle with a paper model first and adjust it as necessary. When all the sawing and filing of the cut-out cells is completed the strip can be shaped into a cylinder ready for soldering. This can be initially formed by hand over a suitably sized rod supported in the vice and then malletted.

Bind the seam if it is slightly springy and solder with paillons if it is broken into lots of short lengths. An unbroken seam can be stick soldered. When the silver has been quenched, cleaned and dried it can be properly formed by mallet. Always check that the glass vessel fits into the cylinder and if it is slightly tight, the cylinder can be tapped on a flared tool if available or very lightly tapped with a planishing hammer. Using a metal hammer on a metal tool surface will always stretch annealed metal, whereas a mallet will only move/stretch the metal a comparatively small amount. Once the glass liner can fit in the pierced silver, it is time to check that the bottom edge is flat and prepare a base. This can be a solid disc of silver or a ready-cut 'donut' shape with a central hole or a circle of chunky wire that fits neatly into the cylinder. Leaving a hole in the middle makes it easier to push the glass out.

The two tabs next to the seam can now be turned to a right angle to the body of the cylinder. This is easily done with flat or snipe nose pliers. Grip the tabs as close to the top of the box as possible and gently fold them out in turn. If the top edge is slightly deformed at this point, tap with a mallet to make sure it is round. The tabs are going to be curled up with round nose pliers to make a tiny closed circle but only one will be soldered. It is important that the circles are truly side-by-side and form a straight line. A short piece of wire or even an old hat pin can be pushed through to check the alignment is true. If the tabs are too long, the loops will be very big and their length should be reduced. Make them to fit the wire pin that will be used for this project, which will be silver wire of around 1.5mm thickness. Turning small pieces of sheet and wire into neat, round curves may look deceptively simple but this really should be practiced on some scrap first to get a feel for the action of the pliers and the behaviour of the metal.

The body of the salt cellar can be set aside now while the top is made. This will also have a tab sticking out, measured to fit exactly between those on the box. If the lid has any patterning or shaping such as a shallow dome, this should be done now. Check that the top sits comfortably on the base and that it lines up properly. Later on there will be a little salt spoon made to go with the salt cellar so a small bite must be cut or filed out of the edge of the lid where it will sit.

Another consideration is how the lid will be lifted open. It could have a little top-knot to act as a handle or a lip at the front to provide an edge to grip. A loop at the front can be made from a tab similar to that being used for the hinge, which will mean there is no additional soldering. A tidy solution to making both a gap for the spoon to sit and a tiny loop handle is to take the saw cuts for the tab into the lid. When the strip of silver is fully curled up it will leave a space for the spoon. This may sound rather fiddly but although it is all on a small scale, it is fairly straightforward.

SALT SPOON

Making the silver salt spoon is not so different from making any other spoon. It could be forged from a smallish chunk of 3mm thick wire or can be made in two parts with a bowl pressed in the doming block and a separately formed handle. The bowl of the spoon is really tiny so need not be any bigger than 10–15mm diameter. To introduce a new technique, the example salt spoon has a twisted handle soldered onto the bowl. Twisted wire can be tricky to control when it comes to filing but in this instance it will be work hardened, which means it is more resistant and therefore less likely to move about. It is really satisfying to twist wire and all sorts of permutations of different twist can be achieved with different profiles of wire.

In this example though the little spoon will just have a length of plain round wire doubled over and twisted with a hand drill. These are used less and less for DIY due to the ease and relative cheapness of electric drills but they are very handy for wire work and still readily available. The thickness of the wire should be between 1mm and 1.5mm thick at the heaviest and around 130mm long. Carefully fold the wire in half and hold the two ends in the bench vice. This last 3–5mm of wire will be held firmly in the vice without the guards, which will leave the ends rather chewed up but these will be chopped off and filed after twisting. The loop that is sticking out is now about 60mm long. Fix a cup hook into the end of the hand drill and slip the loop of wire over it. Pull back just enough to feel a little tension and turn the drill handle to twist the wire up. Turning a small amount will provide an open twist and a couple of turns more will deliver a tight twist. Just stop when you are happy with the result.

Unloop the drill and open the bench vice. The ends of the wire will be mashed up and cannot be rescued but the loop can be left as part of the handle design. Twisted wire rapidly becomes work hardened so if using this technique for other projects, do not overwork the metal but anneal if it is to be hammered flat, for example. Keeping it work hardened at this stage however is an advantage as it will bend less. Saw through double wires, taking care to hold them together if they threaten to separate. File the ends to fit the domed bowl of the spoon and solder in place. If flux flows into the twist then solder will too, so make sure that enough solder is present for it to do the main task of joining the two parts.

A SILVER SALT CELLAR AND SPOON

Tools

- Steel stake for forming cylinder
- Leather or wooden mallet
- Piercing saw
- Centre punch drill
- Hand drill

Materials

- Glass salt liner
- Paper template based on the glass
- Silver sheet 0.8mm–1.0mm (the size will be determined by the size of the glass salt cellar liner)
- Silver disc 10mm diameter for the spoon
- Silver wire approx. 1.2mm x 130mm

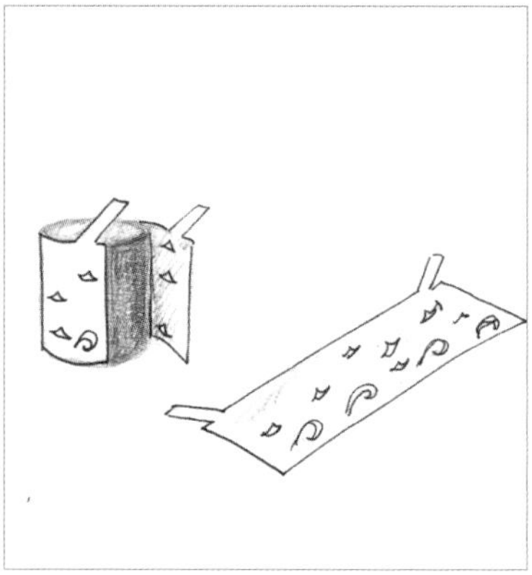

STEP 1 Make a pattern to fit the glass liner and transfer to the silver. Cut out the silver including the tabs that will form the hinge.

STEP 2 Centre punch the site of all the holes and drill them with a 1mm drill. Emery the back of the holes.

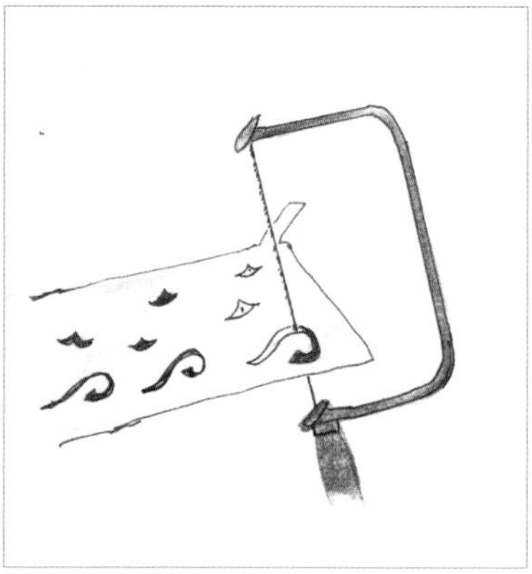

STEP 3 Open one end of the saw and feed the blade into the first hole. Tighten the saw ready to cut out the pattern. Repeat this for each hole in the design.

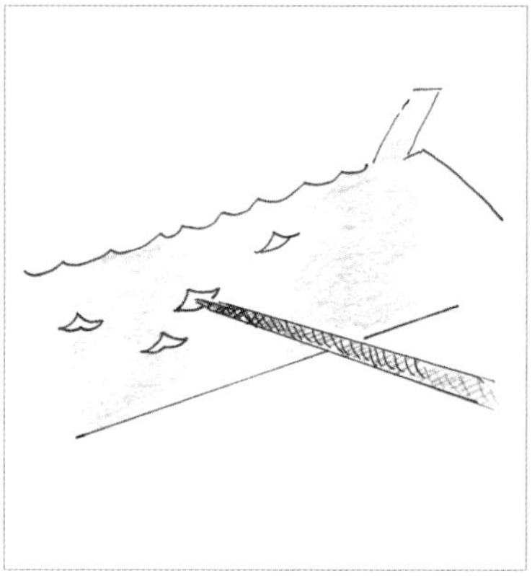

STEP 4 After sawing, file all accessible cut edges including the seam. If the pattern has any wobbles, tidy up the cut-out design with a small needle file.

STEP 5 Shape the sheet into a cylinder on the steel stake. Align the seam and tie with binding wire before soldering.

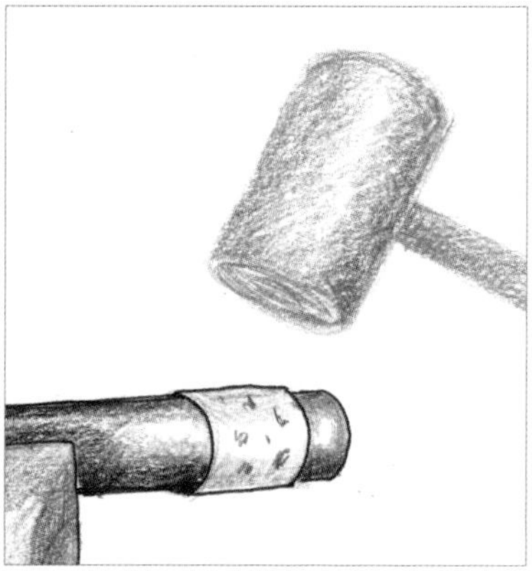

STEP 6 Mallet round on steel rod held in the vice. Prepare a base and solder this on next, pickle rinse and dry.

STEP 7 Use flat pliers to fold the tabs down to a right angle with the cylinder. They will now be parallel to each other. Change to round nose pliers to make the tabs into a curl.

STEP 8 Feed a tight-fitting rod or wire through the loops and adjust so it is evenly aligned. Trim off any excess length. These 'tube' hinges do not have to be soldered. Burnish to harden after assembly is complete.

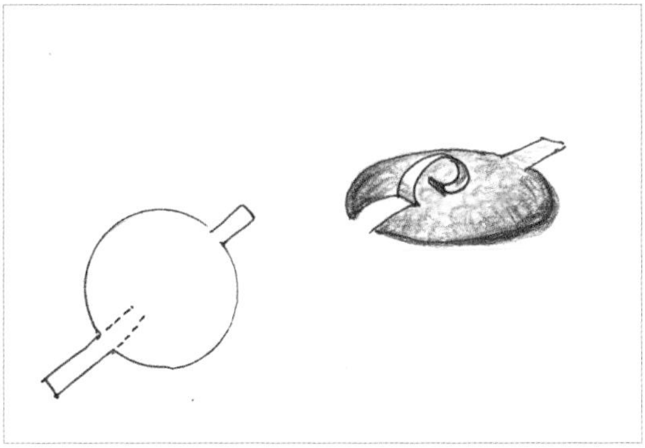

STEP 9 Prepare the lid according to the pattern with the hinge tab, and handle/spoon slot.

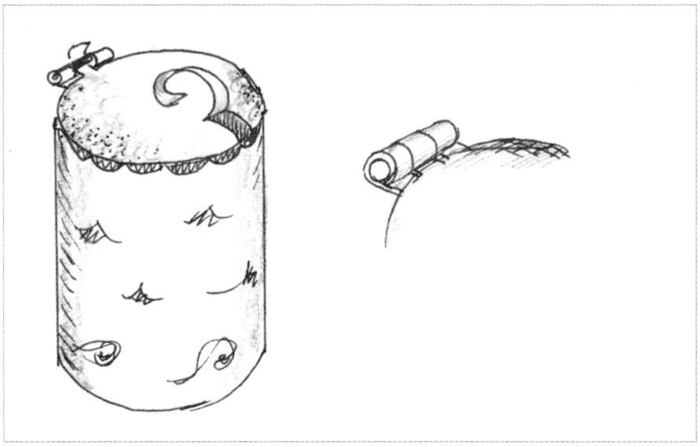

STEP 10 Curve the hinge tab before feeding it under the wire. Use flat pointed pliers to close the tab tightly around the wire. When firmly attached, file the ends of the wire flush.

The salt cellar is completed. The glass liner can be pushed into the pierced out silver container. When the lid is closed there is a small cut out which will fit the salt spoon described below.

Salt spoon

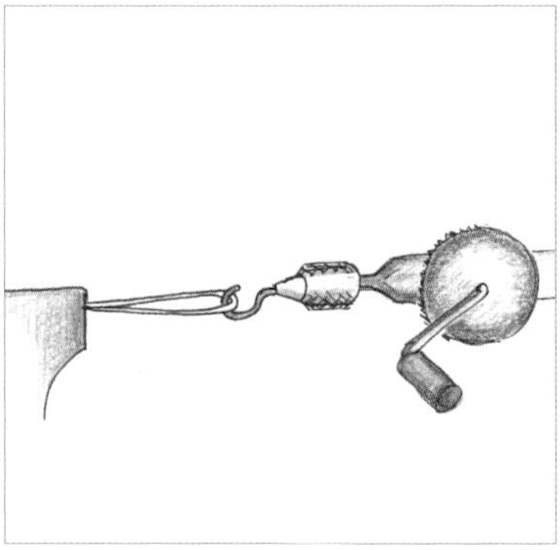

STEP 1 Cut a 130mm length of 1.3mm diameter wire and fold it loosely with the two ends in the vice. Fix a hook in the hand drill and feed this through the loop of wire. Turn the drill handle to twist the wire.

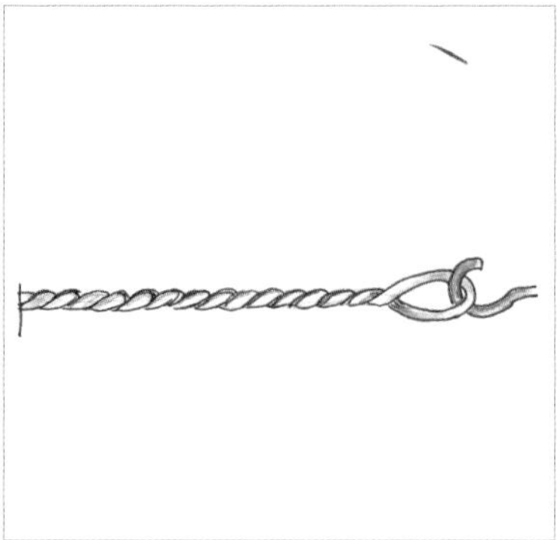

STEP 2 Carefully pull the wire so it is even and turn the handle of the hand drill to twist the wire.

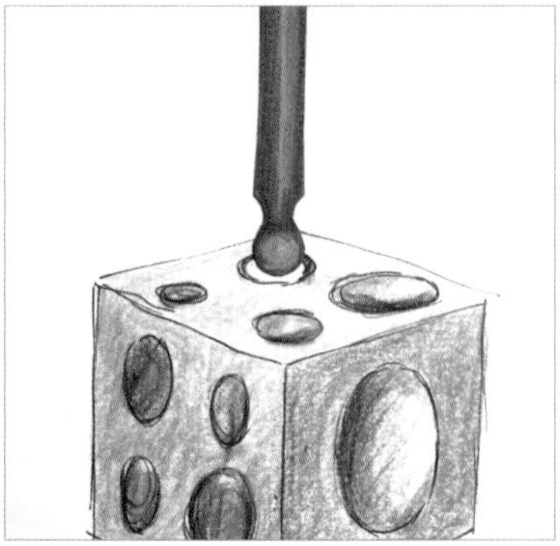

STEP 3 Cut out a small disc of 0.7mm sheet about 13mm diameter, file round and shape in a doming block.

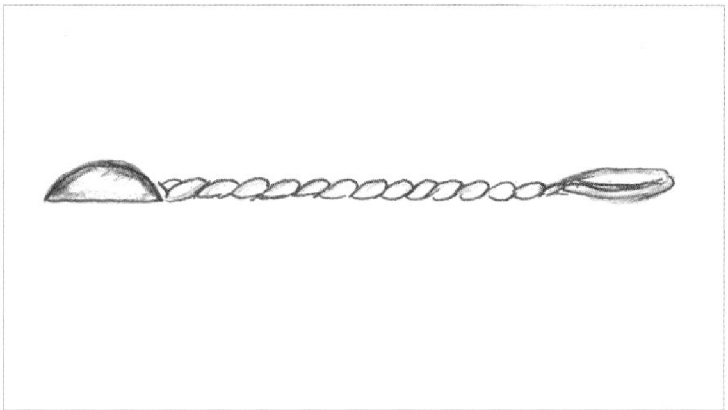

STEP 4 Cut off the rough ends of the twisted wire and file it to fit the profile of the spoon bowl.

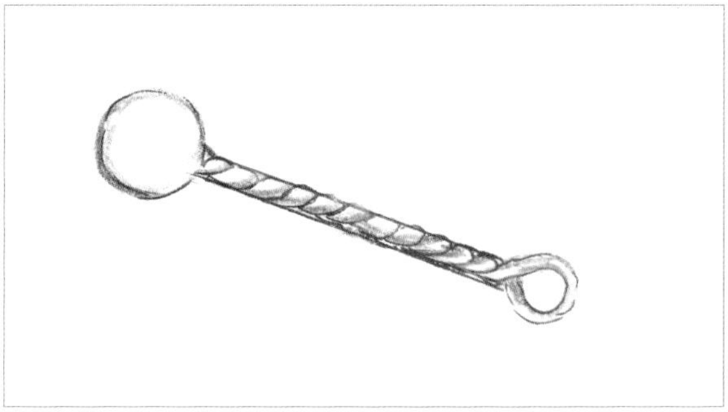

STEP 5 Solder the two parts together, making sure to join both strands of the twisted wire.

This tiny spoon can be polished by hand or with a small motor tool such as a jeweller's pendant motor polisher. It is also suitable for cleaning in a barrel polisher, which is used by jewellers for brightening and hardening small items. This tool is not used in silversmithing as a rule because it is not appropriate for flat surfaces.

HOW TO MAKE CHENIER

Should the need for a length of tube occur and there is none to hand, a description of how to make it is below. It is made from a strip of flat sheet curled up on the shorter side, which means that there will be a seam along its length. This seam can either be soldered up in advance or soldered when it is being attached to something. The long seam is difficult to see once the tube has been drawn down to the desired size so it can be hard to solder correctly. The instructions below are therefore included as an interesting technique to add to a portfolio of useful skills, but not necessarily recommended for use when making a first hinge.

Tools

- Steel ruler
- Dividers
- Steel flat plate
- Swage block and steel rods (old knitting needles or small wooden dowel can be used)
- Small rawhide mallet
- Round draw plate with large holes (from 4mm diameter)
- Draw tongs or heavy general-purpose pliers

Materials

- 8mm sheet x 10mm x 70mm. These dimensions can be adapted for other thicknesses of sheet.

Work from a straight edge of silver and open the dividers to a width of 9 or 10mm. Hold one edge to the side of the silver sheet and draw a straight parallel line about 70mm long.

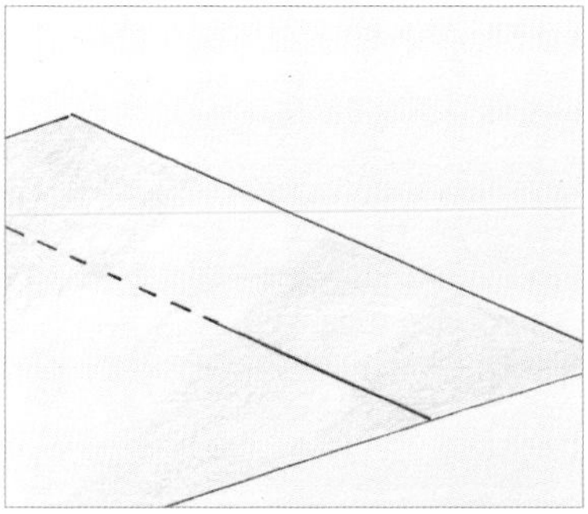

STEP 1 Cut out and file a 9mm strip and shape the last 15mm to a slight taper. File the edges smooth and totally straight so that when curved, the edges meet. Taper the ends so it has the outline of a fat pencil.

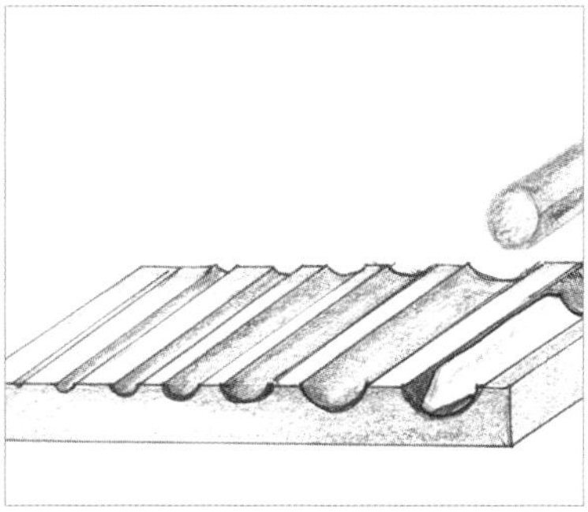

STEP 2 Place the strip of silver in the largest groove of the swage block and use the mallet and rod to press it into the hollow.

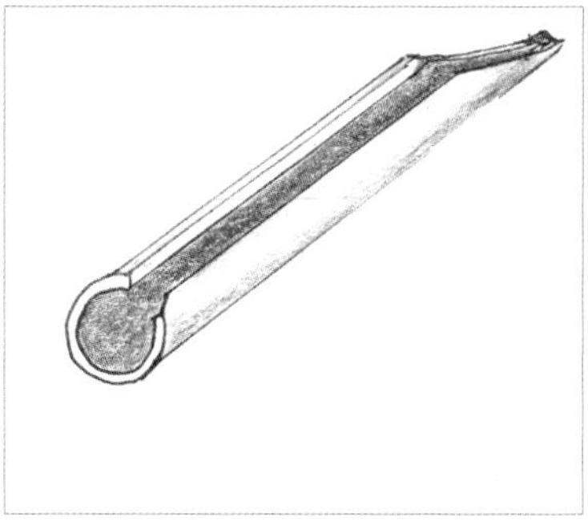

STEP 3 This process is similar to using a doming block, starting large and gradually tapping the strip into narrower grooves until it is the same curve in section as a letter 'c'.

STEP 4 Anneal the curved strip of silver, pickle, rinse and dry. File the edges at a slight inward angle so that they will meet when the form is closed. Lie the curved strip on a flat plate with the opening to one side. Gently tap the edge down with a small mallet working along until the full length is closed. Tap the tapered end closed.

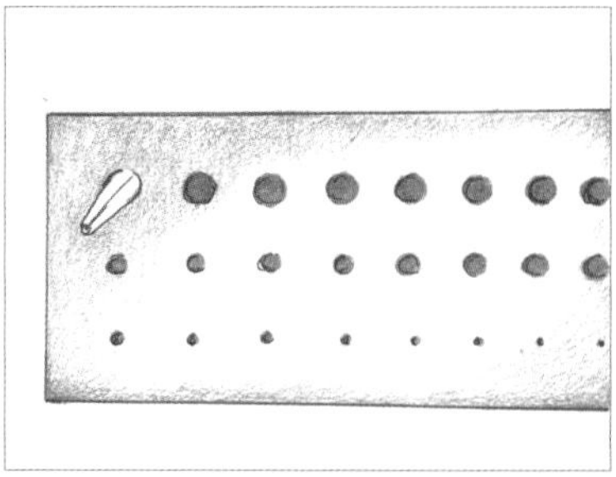

STEP 5 This tube is still too large but it can be reduced in size. The wall thickness will remain the same but the central hole will get smaller. Place the draw plate in the vice or draw bench and feed the tapered end through the largest hole to pull it through. Anneal, clean and dry.

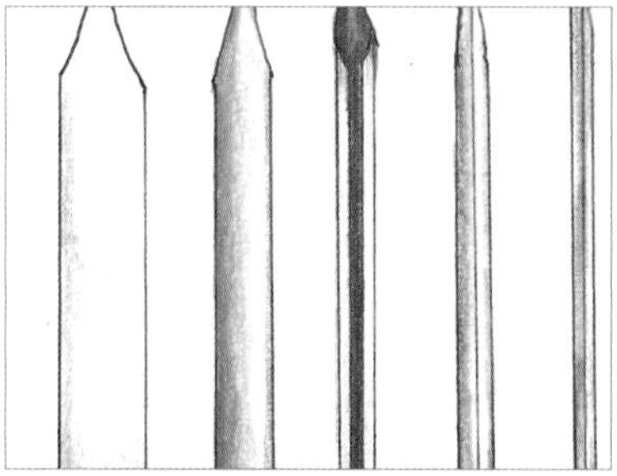

STEP 6 Continue to draw down the length of tube until it is the desired dimension, keeping an eye on the hole as it is this that will diminish rather than the thickness of the tube wall.

The seam can be soldered closed. The tube is now complete and ready to use, just take care when positioning any sections of chenier that the seam along its length is soldered onto a surface and not left exposed.

Hinged containers.

CHAPTER 10

Other Hammering Techniques

RAISING

Raising, like sinking, is used to create three-dimensional hollow or vessel forms. However, the two methods of working silver differ considerably in what they do to the metal as it is worked. Sinking will reduce the gauge or thickness of the metal because hammering it with the ball pein hammer makes the sheet thinner as it is spread and stretched into a new form. By contrast, raising compacts the silver whilst at the same time coaxing it into a new shape. This may sound like an unfeasible proposition but with a reduced outer perimeter but greater depth, the original thickness of the metal should remain the same. Because of this ability to retain an even thickness of metal, raising is used to create deeper forms such as bowls, cups, vases, teapots or trophies. Obviously many vessels could be formed from flat sheet with a soldered side seam, so why bother to spend hours hammering? The answer is that it is an incredibly versatile technique and that those hours of hammering can result in sophisticated forms that cannot be readily achieved by fabrication alone.

A raised beaker.

Raising is one of the oldest techniques of metal forming and really is at the heart of silversmithing because it is based purely on skilled hammer work. There are variants of this hammering technique in metalworking across most cultures of the world, reaching back to the early history of smithing. Transforming a flat piece of metal into a three-dimensional object with no folds or soldered seams is a deeply satisfying experience. Expect the progression from flat sheet to fully formed three-dimensional object to take time and do not try to rush at any stage. Resist the temptation to start on anything bigger than a beaker or cup because this is all about controlling the work; if it is too large it will be harder to hold steady and take a lot longer to see results. Raising will take more than one attempt to perfect so it really is worth trying it in copper or gilding metal first just to understand what is happening.

There are a few points to understand before starting but otherwise this is at its core a fairly simple forming method of compressing the metal in a controlled way over a steel stake.

Start with a profile drawing of the object that is to be raised – this determines the size of blank/flat disc of sheet silver needed. Make a careful measurement of the depth and work out the average width. For a gently flared beaker the average width is neither the top (widest part) nor the bottom (narrowest point) but somewhere around the centre or halfway between the two dimensions.

Add the height and average width measurements together and this gives you the diameter of the blank that will be needed for making the vessel. This formula works pretty well for most tall, rounded or outward flaring shapes because a larger area of the surface is going to be worked. For wide-based vessels of a shallow depth where less of the surface area is going to be hammered, take the sum of the height and the widest point of the profile as the size of blank. (There will be other versions of this formula for working out the size of the blank disc, but this is widely used and has proven to be a pretty good guide.)

Keep the drawing to hand throughout the working process as it will be a guide to the progress of the raising.

Ideally, the thickness of the vessel walls should end up being the same as the silver blank at the outset. If the metal is overly thinned the vessel will be larger than the original design and not much can be done to regain the thickness of the sides, although the height can be trimmed down if it is too tall. When the finished object is noticeably smaller than was originally intended it will mean that the sides of the vessel have been thickened but without being extruded upwards enough. This is a bit easier to remedy, as it just means a little more hammering is needed to enlarge the object until it is a closer match to the original design.

One way of slightly enlarging a vessel is to planish it a couple of extra times. This will only thin the metal very slightly but will increase the overall size so may not be suitable if the rim is the correct diameter, in which case further work with the raising will be needed. Paying attention to the angle of work during the hammering is the best way to ensure that there will be a good outcome. If the angle is too shallow then it will be hard to change the silver enough to progress into a deep three-dimensional form and if the angle is held up from the stake too steeply the raising will be very hard to control, making it lumpy and uneven. What happens when the metal is held at the correct angle of 30 degrees and pushed down with each hammer blow onto the stake is that a ripple or bulge of metal is created. With each progressive circuit of the disc, this bulge is gradually pushed up by the continuous hammering outwards to the top edge. The metal behind that ripple now has a smaller circumference and diameter. This may be hard to visualize in a material like metal but something similar happens on a potter's wheel when the clay is squeezed upwards. If the shaping stops midway, there will be a bulge or flare of material above this line and the same effect is evident during raising.

Accurate raising is as much about the feel of the working process as being visually attuned to what is happening. Just remember that as a beginner it is best to take your time, because this is a fairly physical activity and dependant on consistent hammer work. Stop for a rest if the non-hammering hand starts to tire. For right-handed hammerers the left hand will be holding the metal in precisely the right place during the working process, and vice versa for those who are left handed. Either way, gripping the metal is demanding for extended periods of time and can be quite hard work, as this hand is acting like a vice.

TOOLS

The hammers and stake are the two principal tools used in this process.

The raising stake is either 'T' shaped with the top of the 'T' bar offering two different profiles for working with, or a three-arm stake with a further choice of working end. Both of these tools are designed to provide some variation so that a smith can easily work from a different end for developing a slightly different shape. The two-arm stake is often permanently fixed in a tree trunk but can be held in the vice, whereas the three-arm stake can only be held in a vice for working. Dedicated raising stakes are quite expensive but fortunately not absolutely necessary. A longish steel bar (up to 300mm/1 foot × 50–60mm/2–3 inches or more) can be customized for use as a hammering surface. The working end will need to be slightly flat on top and ground away underneath at an undercut angle. It must be filed, ground down and smoothed so that there are no dents, blemishes or rough surfaces. If using a grinding wheel or old file to achieve the desired shape make sure to clean the work surfaces very carefully afterwards because steel can contaminate the silver. A magnet is an excellent way to remove any hidden traces of steel dust or filings. Emery and polish the working surface to a good shine.

Do not be tempted to use a thinner rod, as it is not recommended to work on anything with a diameter less than 30mm. This is because it will not provide enough of a contact area for effective raising. Small stakes are only used for creating narrower details such as the neck of a vase or carafe. Traditionally, a general-purpose stake would be kept permanently fixed in a tree trunk where the work is carried out from a seated position. However, raising can also be done standing at the bench with the stake held in a sturdy vice. Standing up for hammering can be very comfortable and has the advantage of being able to change stakes fairly quickly. An engineer's vice is usually strong enough to support a stake for long spells of hammering, but an old leg vice is often better. If any vice is not gripping the work sufficiently, the stake will have to be repositioned from time to time so that the correct working height and angle are maintained.

The raising hammer is a specialist tool and one of the 'must haves' for a silversmithing workshop. It is worth investing in a good one as it can be used for other metal-forming projects. It is a type of cross pein hammer with both faces fairly narrow from top to bottom and wider in the horizontal plane, around 25mm/1 inch. One face may be slightly narrower with a more rounded profile; this is frequently used for forging and is not suitable for raising. This is because the more pronounced curve on the cross pein would stretch the metal too much resulting in a larger and thinner finished object. The raising face is somewhat flatter and will form the metal without the thinning effect of the forging face.

A newly purchased raising hammer will need to have edges and corners rounded then smoothed with fine emery paper. It is important that the hammer face is free of blemishes or pitting and is very highly polished to a mirror finish. It is almost impossible to keep the stake and hammer in perfect condition, so take some time to do a little maintenance on the tools either after a project has been finished or before the next one is started.

A blocking hammer has one or two rounded ends and is used to get the form started. It is usually fairly heavy because it is not for extended use. A general-purpose hammer can be used as long as the ball pein is unblemished. The blocking can also be done with a round-ended wooden mallet. A mallet will provide a softer, more diffuse blow so does not mark the work in the process. If the mallet is lighter in weight than a hammer, it will just take a little more time to achieve the same result. This stage of the process is just to make the project a little easier to hold so the forming need only be a minimal curve.

The planishing hammer is used to finish a piece; this is a fairly light- to medium-weight hammer with a flat, highly polished face. Again, a lighter weight general-purpose hammer can be ground and polished for planishing, but it is well worth investing in a dedicated planishing hammer as it will be used in many if not most projects. A new planishing hammer may also need to have any corners or edges softened and polished before being used for the first time. It should be kept polished, so it is important to clean up any blemishes straight away before they are inadvertently transferred to the surface of a newly completed piece of work.

For a novice smith, it makes sense to start working with copper or preferably gilding metal. These metals are widely available and cost a lot less than silver. It is worth doing a trial in base metal, not just because the technique should be mastered before taking the plunge in silver but also to help visualize the end product. It is one thing to read the description and follow instructions carefully but another matter entirely to feel the process as it is happening. This sense of what occurs during raising can best come through the physical experience of the technique.

Once the decision has been made to progress to silver, it can be either Britannia or sterling as both are suitable. The former is softer because of its slightly higher purity but also more expensive than sterling silver. It is less prone to developing firestain which, as previously explained, is the shadow-like mark beneath the surface of the silver caused by the trace of copper becoming more apparent with each anneal. Sterling silver is often covered with an anti-firestain product such as Argotect during annealing that helps to protect it while it is heated. However, due to the potential hazard of the fumes produced it should only be used if the hearth has an efficient extraction system. One alternative is to let sterling silver become covered in firestain during the annealing and accept that the colour of the silver will be subtly darker than if it is polished away. This works well if the raised piece is going to be finished with a planished surface with no filing.

If a smoothed mirror finish is the ultimate goal then any firestain has to be filed, emeried or buffed away. In a project like this there will be a lot of annealing so it is important to remember to achieve the correct temperature over the whole sheet. Too low and the metal will not be softened, too high and it could be damaged by overheating. Keep the light level low near the hearth while annealing and it will be easier to see the metal change colour and become dull red, at which point it should be quenched. Cleaning the metal in the pickle after annealing will leave the surface white and matt, which will help you see where each hammer blow lands when raising resumes.

The method of raising described below starts from the base near the centre of the blank and gradually works out towards the perimeter of the circular disc. The hammering is done in concentric circles starting from the base working up to the full height or outer edge of the piece – this is known as a 'course' of hammering. To keep on track, concentric circles can be drawn onto the surface after annealing but before the next course of work begins. It is best to use a pencil for this rather than a scribe or dividers, as pencil marks will not affect the integrity of the metal's surface.

This is a commonly practiced method of raising, but it is not the only way to raise a vessel. As with so many traditions there are variations within the broad methodology but for simplicity the following 'centre outwards' method is the one described. Raising is a gradual process so the outer circumference will decrease slowly bit by bit. Don't try to do too much at once but rather aim to make steady progress in reducing the size by 5–8mm each time. With experience this technique does get faster and more accurate, but for beginners it is important to take it easy and concentrate on correctly placing each hammer blow.

Health and safety

There are few specific health and safety issues with raising other than the usual good workshop practice, in particular around the hearth. Tiredness and posture are more likely to be an issue if this is the first attempt at this technique. It does demand time and concentration whilst holding the work firmly in position so whether standing at a bench vice or seated at a tree trunk, take a break to stretch the back and shoulders, flex the fingers and shake out the hammering arm as needed. Don't expect to see quick results in the beginning but instead enjoy the incremental steps on the journey from flat disc of silver to a fully formed three-dimensional object.

Hammering is a percussive action, which will work best when the metal that is being formed is held in the correct position while it is being struck. If it becomes uncomfortable holding the metal, protect the fingers with tape or wear a well-fitting glove to shield the gripping hand. For comfort as well as good health and safety practice, always wear ear defenders for extended periods of hammering. The sound from the hammering can be muted by ear defenders but is not totally blocked out. This allows the timbre of each strike to be heard and judged; it should be a sharp ringing blow, which confirms that the copper or silver has been struck onto the steel surface of the stake.

MAKE A DRINKING BEAKER

Tools
- Dividers and compass and marker pen/pencil
- Steel ruler and calipers for measuring
- Piercing saw
- Hand files, emery paper and burnisher
- Round-ended wooden mallet or blocking hammer
- Flat wooden or rawhide mallet
- Sandbag or wooden former for blocking
- Raising hammer
- Planishing hammer
- Raising stake or customized steel bar
- Wooden dowel or flat-ended rod/stake

Materials
- 1mm thick sheet of silver/copper cut into a circle

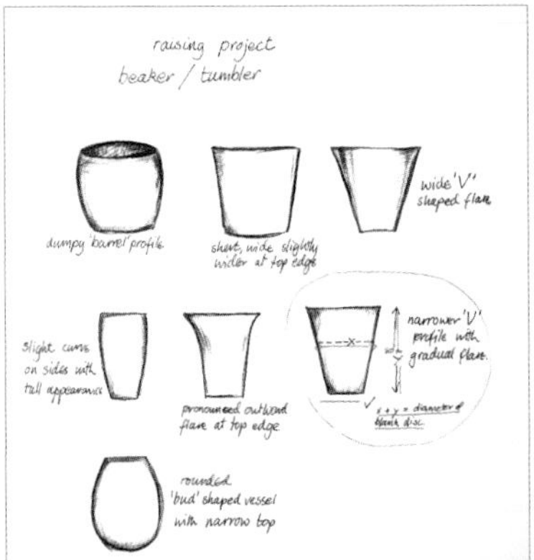

STEP 1 Draw the design in profile; this will be a point of reference throughout the project. Measure the drawing and mark the height and the average width. The sum of these provides the diameter of the blank disc.

STEP 2 Clean the silver and use a compass and marker pen to draw the base outline, followed by concentric circles 10mm apart out to the edge of the circle.

STEP 3 Cut out a disc and place it on the sandbag or the shallow wooden former and mallet or 'block' the disc into a shallow hollow. Continue until this is an evenly distributed curve then anneal. It is possible to skip this stage and start with a flat disc but the introduction of a slight hollow makes this much easier to hold, particularly with larger objects.

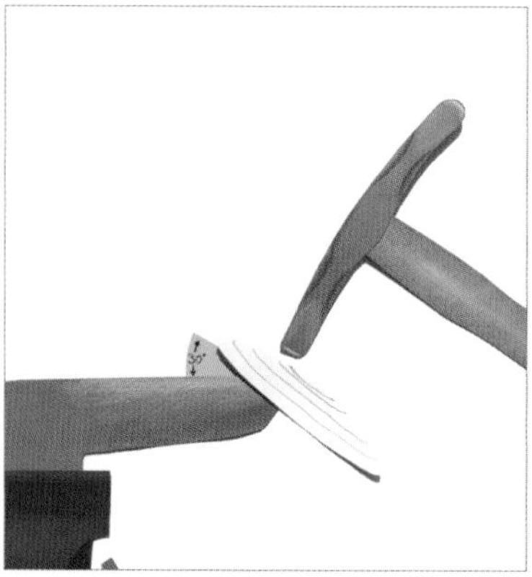

STEP 4 Put the stake or steel bar into the engineer's vice, making sure it is held securely in a horizontal position. Start at the first circle from the base, hold the silver firmly at a 30-degree angle with one hand and with the raising hammer, strike the metal onto the stake. Start hammering from the innermost circle.

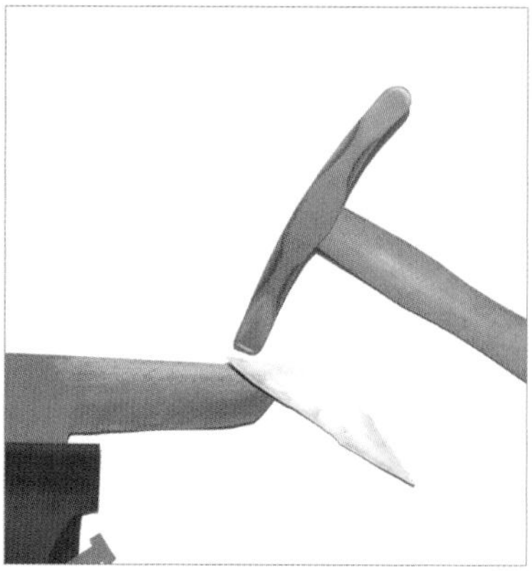

STEP 5 Move the disc round gradually while continuing to hammer the sheet down onto the stake surface. Try to keep to the angle of 30 degrees and if needed, cut a cardboard template to help stay on track. Continue hammering to the last outer circle.

STEP 6 Redraw the guidelines after each anneal and clean. They should be at an even distance to keep the hammering regularly distributed around the surface.

STEP 7 Lightly mallet the annealed form on the stake to keep it in a regular shape. This should not work-harden the metal. This gentle reforming with a mallet is called 'bouging' (from the French verb 'bouger', to move).

STEP 8 Tap the form over a flat-ended wood or metal rod to define the baseline.

STEP 9 After the first circle, slide the metal back to the end of the stake so that the second round of hammering starts at the same point. A ridge in the metal may appear but as the metal is hammered round, this ripple will be moved upwards with each circuit of hammering.

STEP 10 Continue to hammer at the same angle all round up to the outer edge, keeping the hammer blows overlapping and close together so that the raising is even.

STEP 11 The top circumference and diameter will continue to decrease with each course of working while the height becomes greater. Take as many courses of raising as needed to achieve the desired final shape and remember to anneal and clean after each one.

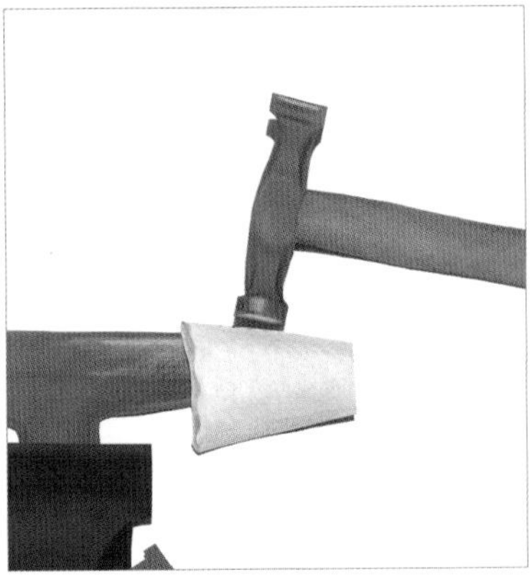

STEP 12 Planishing is done on the raising stake or other suitable smooth-surfaced stake. Use the planishing hammer with quick, light and overlapping taps that even out all previous hammer marks. If one course is not enough then anneal, clean and repeat the process.

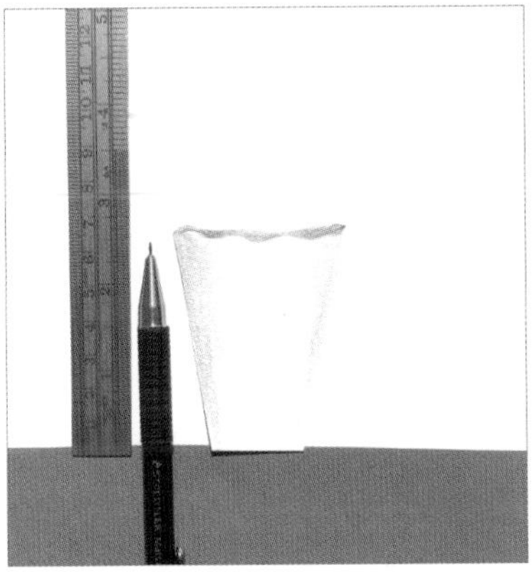

STEP 13 Even with regular caulking around the top edge, it may not be absolutely flat. The height should be checked and marked with a surface gauge or ruler.

STEP 14 The top edge can be filed down or if it is very uneven, it can be trimmed down to the lowest point with shears rather than sawing. Only cut in an anticlockwise direction to avoid damaging the edge.

STEP 15 The top edge can be given a final caulk to thicken it up and add an attractive shimmer to the rim. Caulking can be done over the last few courses of raising if the edge is fairly even; this builds the thickness of the rim.

The whole piece has now been formed and given the final planish, so it can be lightly buffed by hand to leave the hammered finish. If the design calls for a smooth polished surface, it will need further work with abrasives before the final polish.

As mentioned above, if it is absolutely necessary to tidy up an uneven edge it can be cut down with shears to remove the excess. The reason for only cutting in an anticlockwise direction is to ensure that the shears do not veer off in a diagonal direction, which would damage the work. Ideally the edge should not need this but for a first attempt it is useful to know how it can be remedied. With each course of hammering, the bulge of metal is pushed outwards making the rim appear flared. This slightly flared edge is the remains of the ripple of metal that has been gradually eased up the sides of the vessel. To avoid any risk of creating a fold or pleat in the metal, it can be malletted onto the stake instead of using a hammer for the very top edge before annealing. In this way the edge should be kept even without being stressed throughout the raising right up to the last circuit of forming. Other than an uneven edge or cracks caused by pleating, there are not too many major disasters that can happen with a raising project. As long as the normal rules of not overworking or overheating the metal are followed, this can be avoided.

Raising is one of the fundamental techniques of silversmithing and as such it will probably take a few attempts to really get to grips with its full potential. The written description may make it sound more complex than it really is, but in essence raising is not complicated so much as physically demanding. Trying this technique with base metal first will allow the theoretical to fall into place and once this has been experienced, the technique can be improved and worked in silver.

Raising is used to make a range of shapes and of course they do not have to have a straight profile like the project above, which shows how to make a more or less 'v' shape. Many objects have full, rounded curves as well as forms that curve back in on themselves. For the beaker project, each course of hammering began at the same point taking the shape from the base. To make a vessel with a rounded profile, the starting point for a course of hammering can be varied. The shaping is started from the base, which establishes the point at which the object moves from the horizontal plane. Further courses of hammering can start from a level above the base line. Starting the raising halfway up the side means that the lower portion will retain the same angle of elevation, whereas the upper part will be drawn in more. Further starting points higher up the side can be introduced nearer to the top. This means that the form will be drawn in again from a higher point but will leave the rest of the shape unchanged.

After courses of hammering that begin at a higher level above the base, it can appear that a corner or ledge has been created. This is easily malletted away over a rounded stake after annealing, allowing for a more accurate judgement of the form. Checking with the design is crucial with this type of raising as this will determine where the next course of hammering can begin.

The shape of a vessel will in part be determined by the available tools for the job. As long as a stake can accommodate the changing angles and curves, an object can be made by raising. There are small planishing stakes that can fit onto a 'T'-shaped stake extension or inside hollow forms for finishing a rounded piece. An object can be formed on a raising stake then finished on a smaller, dedicated planishing stake that fits inside the form, allowing any irregularities to be removed from the surface.

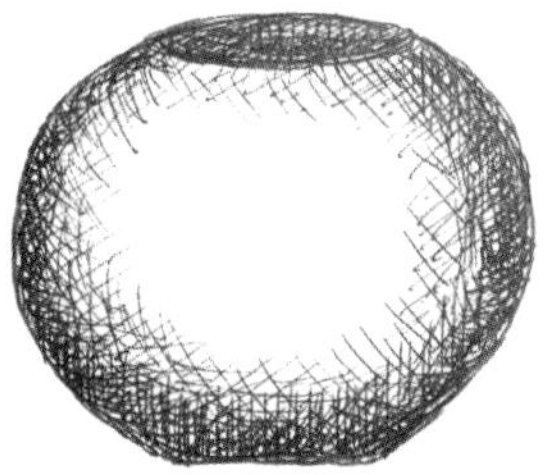

It is possible to raise a rounded form from flat sheet.

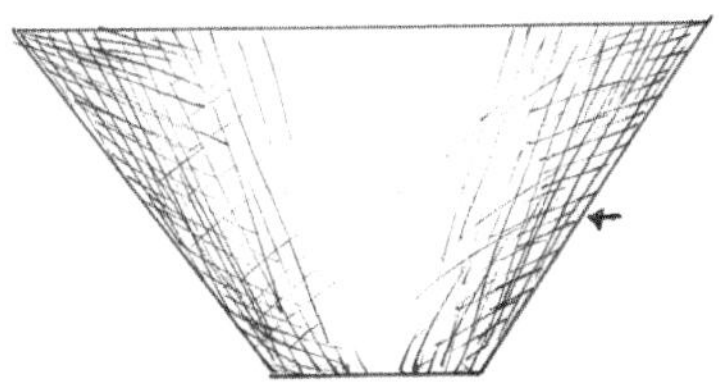

The first few courses of hammering create an even 'v'-shaped flare.

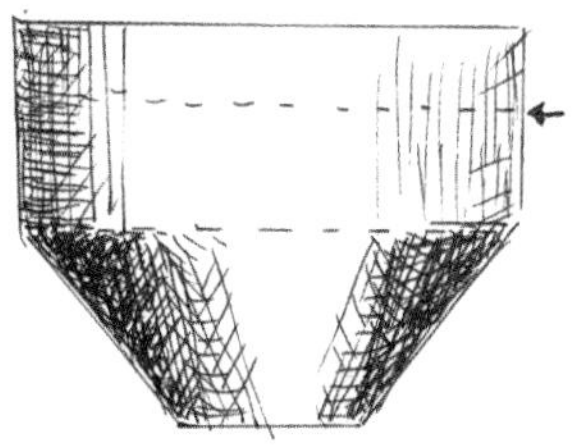

Raising then starts from higher up the side of the vessel.

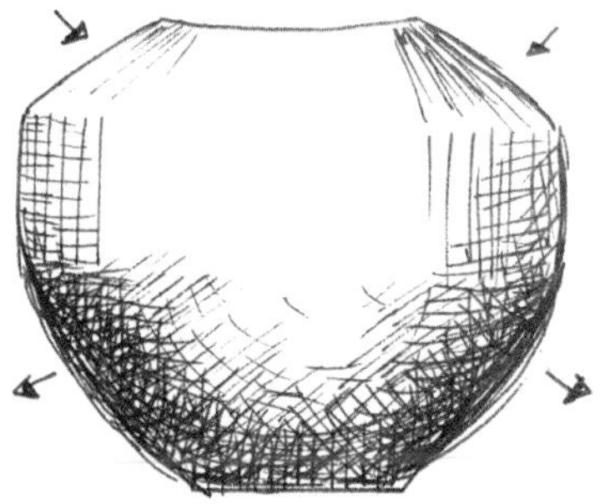

A second higher start line will just work the top third of the vessel.

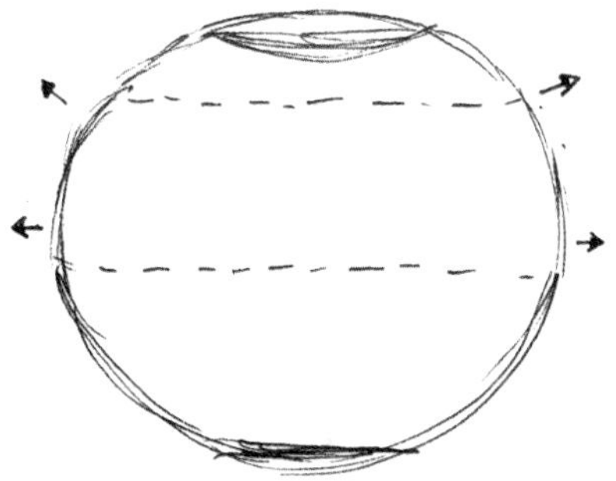

The vessel is planished round on a curved stake to remove any corners or ridges.

Once confident with raising, it can be used to create a variety of shapes by starting to hammer from a level higher than the base, once the sides have been established. In this way the top edge can be drawn in and narrowed to be a smaller aperture than the widest point of the vessel, creating squat or near spherical forms. Mastering raising is a standard silversmithing skill and although there are alternative methods for creating hollow forms, this particular method will always be prized because it is mysterious. The transformation from flat disc of silver into a unique vessel with depth and dimension really is a form of magic, but this alternative sleight of hand happens gradually over time rather than in the blink of an eye. Pour yourself a celebratory drink to toast all the hard work and perseverance in producing a raised vessel.

CHAPTER 11

Constructing a Seamed Vessel or Container

Raising is a versatile technique for creating a large range of hollow vessel forms but three-dimensional objects and vessels can be fabricated from sheet with one or more parts soldered together along a seam. Creating things that have to fit properly can seem like an unnecessary problem to deliberately choose, but this method of construction has the advantage that it may be quicker than raising from flat and has the potential for surface decoration to be built into the piece from the start such as etching or pressing. This different approach to making an object so that it is constructed rather than hammered from flat is widely used because of the advantage of relative speed. There is also a huge variety of shapes that can be achieved using a combination of forming and soldering in their construction.

Seamed vessel.

As with all the silversmithing projects discussed so far there will be pros and cons and in this technique, it is the effort and care taken to create well-fitting seams that is the key to success. In a project that calls for one or more longish seams it is paramount that they must be made to match accurately along the entire length. It will always take a little time to ensure that parts to be soldered are properly prepared to really fit but apart from cutting out the sheet and doing the required shaping, this can be an efficient method of creating an object.

For a first experience of making a seamed vessel, base the project on a forming tool such as a bangle mandrel for a truncated cone or large diameter bar for a cylindrical vessel. Using a former is essential because it allows the piece to be made to particular measurements. The example piece for this project is an up-ended cone with the smaller dimension as the base so that the wider top cut at an angle forms a spout. As an extension to the main theme of a seamed vessel, a handle has been added. Making a handle is an opportunity for design ideas and to create something that is complementary to the proposed form. It is also a chance to revisit forging as described in the chapter on spoon making. Forging is an excellent way to make a structurally useful addition to the piece, but also opens up aesthetic possibilities.

The pictured jug has a handle constructed from sheet, which is an anticlastic curve. An anticlastic form is one that curves in two different planes or axes at once. (A synclastic curve is where the curves are in the same axes, such as a bowl.) An anticlastic curve is a 'u' shape, but curved lengthwise at the same time so that the 'u'-shaped channel is not straight like an open length of tube, but arced.

This new technique is explained later in the chapter and is an interesting addition to hammer forming skills.

The project in this chapter is the construction of a jug or vase formed over a bangle mandrel, or the tapered end of an anvil or other large gradually tapering stake. It is made from one piece to form a round section truncated cone with a side seam and a soldered base, with an optional handle for a jug. If preferred, this project can be made as a straight-sided cylindrical form in which case the pattern will be very easy to make, just allow enough extra in the circumference so that the metal does not fit too tightly on the former. Where a vessel is a conical or flared shape the pattern must reflect this by being an arc to account for one longer edge, either the top or bottom. If using basic geometry or mathematics causes alarm to those not so comfortable with crunching numbers, do not despair, it is possible to make an accurate pattern directly from the mandrel. As with making a rectangular pattern for a cylindrical form, always allow extra width so that the soldered vessel does not fit too snugly on the former. Obviously on a conical vessel, this would just sit further along the former and mean the finished piece is a bit smaller than intended.

CREATING THE PATTERN

To make a pattern, wrap paper around the mandrel and tape it together. This tool is a tapered shape so the wrapped paper will overlap somewhat diagonally with the top and bottom edges pointing up or down. Tape the paper together so that it does not unravel and carefully mark a horizontal line for the top and base edges. Remove the taped conical paper model from the mandrel and carefully cut the top and base edges to make the model the correct height, then gently flatten the pattern. Cut through one of the flattened edges. A correctly aligned vertical line will take the shortest route from top to bottom, running down the side of the vessel. The paper pattern at this stage may look rather crude but the essentials are all there; make a neat copy by drawing around the first draft. Tape the paper together to check that the seam is truly vertical and that the pattern stands upright rather than at a jaunty angle. It should also fit easily on the mandrel. Adjust the pattern as needed until it is absolutely perfect, because it is a lot quicker and cheaper to do this in paper rather than metal.

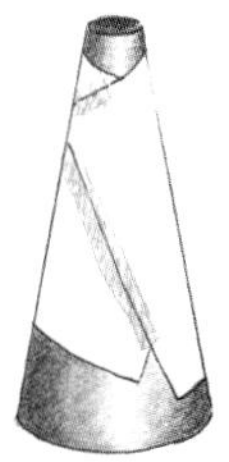

Tape paper around a mandrel.

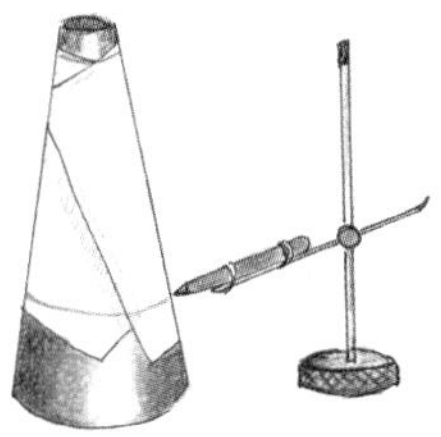

Mark a horizontal line for the base.

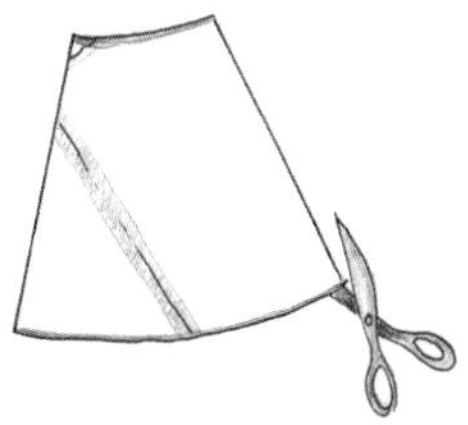

Take the model off the former, trim the base then cut up one side.

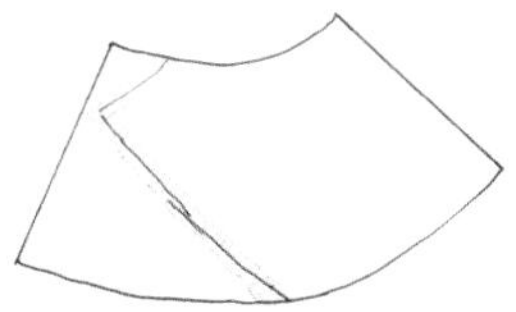

Open out the paper to reveal the template.

This simple method is a quick way to make a pattern, which can be adapted fairly easily. With all larger projects it is strongly recommended that a copper 'mock up' is made before committing to an expensive piece of silver. Keeping notes about the amounts of copper used will also help to determine the costs and time needed for the same project in silver. Because this shape is not a rectangle, it will need a larger sheet of metal to accommodate it and there will be some oddly shaped offcuts. These can come in useful so having a system of separating small scrap from larger pieces is a good way of keeping track of the usable metal available.

MAKE A PARALLEL OR FLARED VESSEL

The steps below can be used for a truncated cone-shape of vessel or a parallel-sided tubular form.

The methods are very similar for each and as always with objects that involve a longer seam, the pieces must be a good fit to ensure that the soldering goes according to plan. It is worth stating again that silver solder will not really fill any gaps and both sides must be touching through the thickness of the metal – that means touching inside and outside. This may sound obvious but with thicker sheet, the angle at which the edges are filed is important to ensure the seam touches along the length and through the thickness of the wall. Stick feeding the solder should ensure flow along the entire length of the seam but do not worry if it isn't quite perfect, as solder can be reapplied to any areas that have not been reached first time. Remember to be disciplined about not introducing the stick of solder before the object is hot enough to accept it, otherwise the solder will melt into a blob and stick to the tweezers. For longer seams, prepare a couple of lengths ready to use just in case one piece is not enough. Always scrape or quickly emery the solder so it is clean and bright before liberally applying flux. A well-prepared piece of solder will help ensure an even flow when molten. The seam will need to be held in contact with binding wire at two or more places along its length. This is pretty straightforward with cylindrical vessels, but conical forms will need a couple of looped lengths to keep the horizontal wires in place.

There are two methods of soldering a base onto the body of the vessel. The first and easier method is to cut out the base, allowing a little extra all round, about 0.5mm–1mm. The body of the vessel will sit on the base to be soldered. This is fairly straightforward to set up and solder but the seam may be just visible after polishing. The second method is slower to prepare because the base is very carefully cut to size and filed to fit into the end of the vessel. The inner wall of the vessel is filed at an inward angle and the base plate edge is chamfered to neatly match, so that it just fits into the vessel. This seam, although slow to fit, will be virtually invisible. After the base plate is soldered to the vessel the piece may be finished. Remember, if the design has a larger base than top then it cannot be worked on the mandrel after soldering the base. In this instance make sure the form needs no further shaping, although it may be possible to mallet or planish on a parallel rod.

Where the base is wide enough it can be an enhancing feature to add a chunky foot wire just inside the outer edge. This is made from a thick rectangular wire about 4mm deep, soldered into a circle before being soldered onto the base. It will create a subtle shadow and give the object a lift to just float above the surface on which it stands.

Health and safety

There are no particular health and safety concerns with this project – as always when soldering there should be proper ventilation at the hearth and tools should be fixed securely at a comfortable height for working. It is always safer to allow enough time to complete each stage without rushing. Working accurately is demanding of concentration; however it is easy to lose oneself in a project so always make sure to take a short break, to rest the eyes and hands to stay comfortably focused.

Tools
- A bangle mandrel, large tapered stake or straight/cylindrical steel rod
- Wooden or weighted rubber 'dead weight' mallet
- Files
- Emery and polishing equipment
- Large dividers
- Piercing saw
- An accurate design on paper and model
- An accurate template

Materials
- Sheet silver/gilding metal/copper

STEP 1 Draw the design out in profile marking the centre line to make a pattern (this will be ×3.14 wider to provide the full circumference but if the maths is too daunting, make a pattern as described above).

STEP 2 Transfer the pattern onto the copper/silver sheet and saw out accurately. Then file the seam edges straight. They may need a slight inward angle to allow for the curvature of the form.

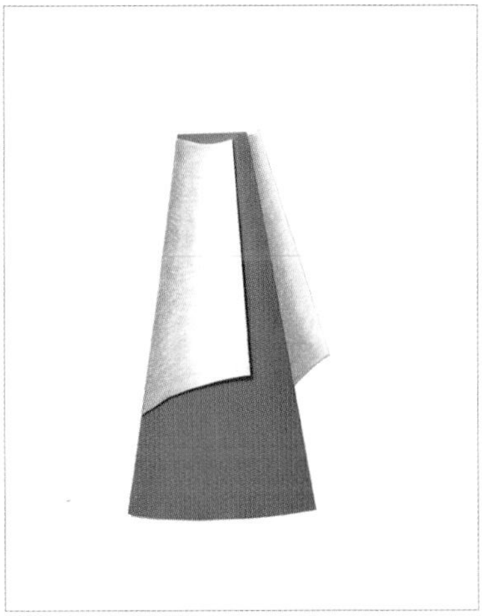

STEP 3 Carefully press the silver sheet onto the former. This can be done by hand and finished with gentle malletting.

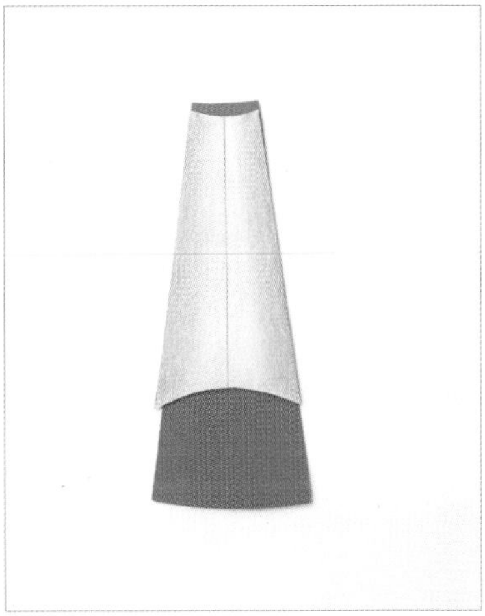

STEP 4 The vessel need not be exactly round as it can be tapped into shape with a mallet after soldering, but the top and bottom edges must be correctly aligned so the side seam is truly vertical.

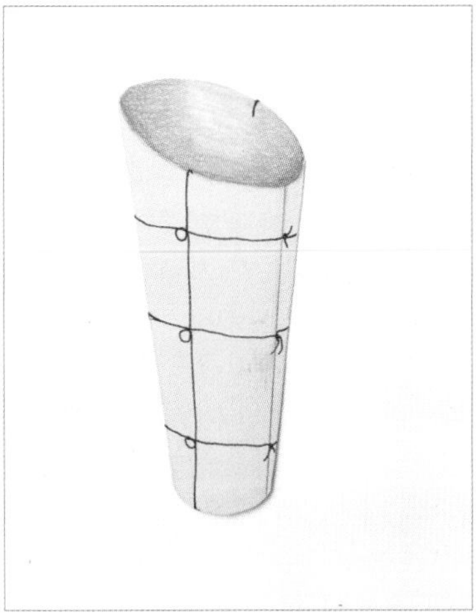

STEP 5 Flared shapes need two vertical looped wires to keep the horizontal binding from slipping. Flux the prepared seam before it is tied together with binding wire. Do not over-tighten the wire.

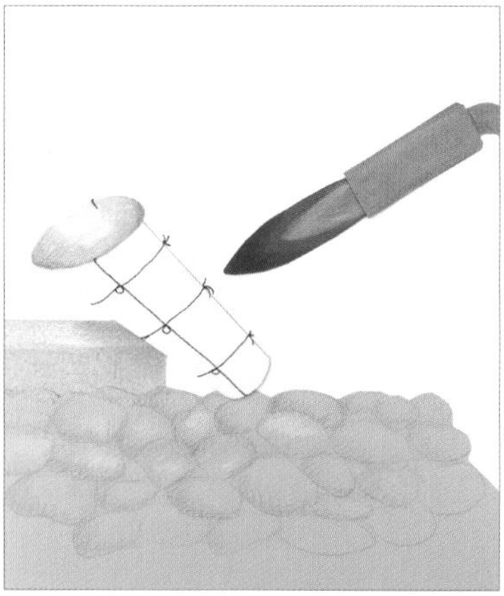

STEP 6 Use plenty of flux on the seam, heat the piece thoroughly and when hot enough introduce the solder. A snippet on the seam will indicate when this temperature is reached.

STEP 7 Remove any binding wire before cleaning in the pickle. Shape the soldered form on the mandrel or rod with a mallet.

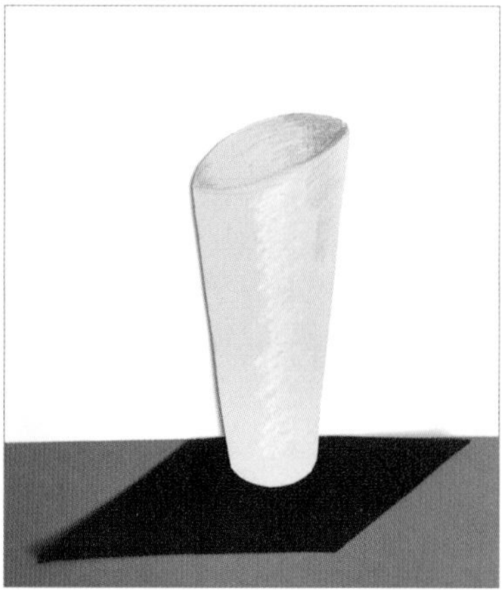

STEP 8 Cut out the base sheet then file and emery the bottom edge of the vessel so that it stands vertically.

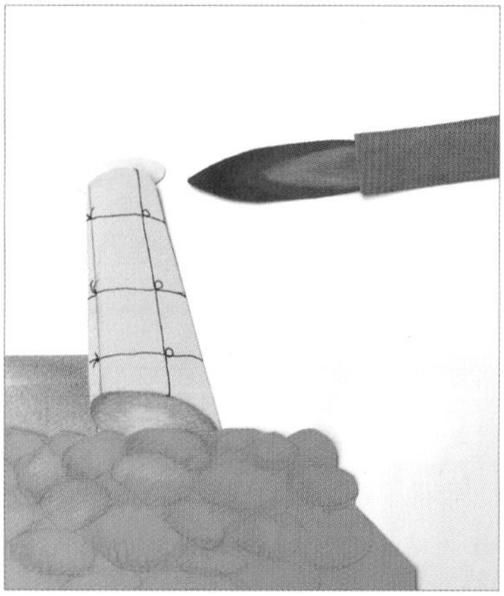

STEP 9 Use binding wire to secure the first seam. Set the fluxed vessel so it can be heated evenly and solder on the base.

STEP 10 Trim off any excess material from the base and file it in line with the side.

The basic form is now complete. The structure can be finished with any further filing and emerying before being polished. If the object is now complete, finish the entire surface but if a handle is to be added just polish this area. It is almost impossible to get a beautiful surface underneath the handle after it is joined onto the body of the vessel, so take time to do this part before making a handle.

The demonstration below is an introduction to a new technique called anticlastic raising. Obviously a handle must be fabricated, finished and filed to fit before being soldered on. As always hold it securely in place with binding wire and use easy solder for this final seam.

MAKING AN ANTICLASTIC HANDLE

This technique is used like forging to create very fluid curved structures. The protected inner part of the curve can be used as a decorative opportunity, as well as structurally in some projects. Anticlastic forming is done using a dedicated stake that has a rather serpentine wiggling shape called a 'sinusoidal' stake. It is an expensive tool to buy for a single project or an experiment, but it is possible to make a carved piece of hardwood or MDF at least 25mm/1in thick with a small 25mm/1in bite carved out of it. This trough or groove should have rounded edges, onto which the metal will be hammered.

To form a 20–30mm strip into an anticlastic shape for a handle, cut the required length and curve it longitudinally. Secure the stake or tool firmly in a vice and hold the ends of the curved strip while it is hammered.

Use a forging or cross pein hammer to tap along the inside of the edge. Work along the strip, keeping the hammer blows overlapping to avoid uneven lumps and bumps. Turn the piece around and repeat the same process along the other inside edge, keeping the hammer blows at a right angle to the surface when it is struck. The next row of hammering will be just inside the first and again repeated on the other side while the curvature is held in place. Over a few rows of hammering, the metal strip is gradually pushed into the trough. In spite of being made from a thinner section of sheet this form will be a fairly strong shape because of these complex curves. It can be annealed and manipulated into the correct shape before the ends are filed to fit the profile of the vessel, ready to be soldered on.

As with all the techniques mentioned in this book, each one can become a specialism in its own right and through trying out tests in copper it will become apparent which are worth revisiting for more in-depth development.

STEP 1 The handle is made from a strip of sheet cut to length. Hold the ends to form an arc while hammering along the length of the outside edge.

STEP 2 Hammer from end to end in rows over the full width to press the curved strip into the hollow. Hold the ends of the strip to maintain the curved shape while it is tapped into the groove.

STEP 3 File the ends of the handle to fit the sides of the vessel and use easy solder for this final joint. Make sure that the handle is held in place securely with binding wire.

FURTHER DEVELOPMENTS OF SEAMED VESSELS

The above example of a seamed vessel uses just one piece of silver to shape the body by being wrapped around a form and soldered to create a tubular structure. This is the simplest approach for making a constructed vessel as there is only one main sheet of metal to be formed with the addition of a base. It is possible to create objects with different profiles by using formed pieces of sheet, which are then joined together with the addition of the base.

The easiest example would be to use a readily available former, such as a hollow wooden bowl former. This allows the structure to be something slightly different from the equally formed vessels that are made from one single formed part, by using two shallower pressed pieces. This new shape from two shallow curves put together can be used vertically or horizontally. Think of putting two cupped hands together to visualize how the seam on such a form would follow the outline of the piece, which can be used for a flask or vase. This type of constructed form can be turned on its side to have a horizontal seam to create a lower but wider form, resembling a flying saucer. Either orientation will need a base and a top opening, so such forms need to have the practical considerations resolved at the design stage.

Hollow objects such as these that are made in pre-formed or pressed parts cannot always be altered or planished after soldering, which means that thinking through the design and making a small-scale test piece will resolve any problems. An arc or dome is a strong shape but the shallower the form is, the more vulnerable it may be, so any dent could really spoil an object that cannot be 'saved' by working on a stake or former if one cannot fit inside after construction. Therefore take care at the finishing and polishing stage so that no excess pressure is used on vulnerable hollow forms.

There are methods of making multi-part vessels with the potential for a larger internal capacity by using unequal parts that differ in depth or profile. Flat planes

Examples of seamed vessel forms.

can also be joined to curved or domed pieces for added volume. With any constructed vessel, the only proviso is that the seams must comfortably meet to seal the structure by some means. In this way flat and curved planes can be introduced into a design, opening up a multitude of further design possibilities. Pressing sheet metal into a bespoke mould allows the smith to produce unusual forms that are not otherwise possible. The compression of sheet into a former is relatively easy and if there is access to a fly press or hydraulic press, it will only take a minute. The main element of making pressed forms is to make the mould in the first place and it is this that takes time and careful planning. Once a mould or die has been made, then multiple repeat forms can be pressed from the same tooling. This area of constructing objects from a mould offers lots of possibilities for experimentation and as with all the techniques touched on so far, it can become a whole area of study in its own right.

Seamed raising is an advanced version of making a seamed vessel. In this technique there is just one main piece of silver as described in the step-by-step guide. The major difference is that seamed raising combines two disciplines, allowing curves to be worked into the soldered object. This brings its own complexity but has the advantage of making the basic three-dimensional form fairly quickly from a flat sheet. The piece would start as a simple cone or cylinder as described earlier, but which is then worked with a raising hammer on suitably shaped stakes to introduce curves. In such an instance, the side seam is prepared in a slightly different way than in a normally constructed vessel.

The first main difference comes after the blank has been cut out and has been filed to size. Mark one side of the sheet as the inside and keep the flat sheet in the vice. The seam is repeatedly tapped with the corner or rounded edge of a file at a slight angle, to match the angle at which the seam will join. This action is similar to an edge being 'caulked' by hammer, but instead it is with the corner or edge of a file. Do not use a sharply cornered file as this could cut too deeply into the edge of the sheet. The purpose of this tapping along each side is that the metal becomes slightly thickened, as it would when caulking with a hammer. The spread out edges provide a greater area of contact along the seam and because it has also been roughened by the edge of the file, it provides a 'key' to create an even stronger bond. This method of edge-thickening is a useful tip to know because it can be applied in other circumstances where a seam might become vulnerable during construction or at some later stage.

The second difference is the shape of the object when it is soldered. Normally edges are aligned so that the piece is more or less round in cross section. In this version of seamed raising, the object will be more of a fat teardrop in cross section. This shape echoes the angle of the filed and roughly tapped edge with more contact than would normally be the case. The final difference with this seam is that 'hard' solder is not used. It is usually appropriate for the first joints in constructed objects but the demands placed on the seams by repeated hammering mean that a higher temperature solder must be used.

Enamelling solder, as its name implies, is used when an enamelled object has some soldered attachment or detail. The fusing temperature of enamel is similar to that of regular hard solder, so any seam that is able to withstand the heat of a kiln or firing temperature for enamel must be a higher temperature solder.

This higher temperature enamelling solder is used when making raised seamed vessels because it allows for multiple anneals to take place without compromising the main seam while the piece is hammered into a new profile. One caveat of this technique is that the availability of appropriately shaped stakes should be checked before embarking on a design. So far this is an open-ended form, which means that the base will have to be added once the raising and planishing has been completed. Normal hard solder can be used for the base seam and if a wire to raise the base is added, this can be soldered in place with easy solder. This combination of techniques is much quicker than raising from a flat sheet and allows the designer to introduce curves into an otherwise straight profile.

SEAMED AND RAISED VESSEL

Seamed raising is a more advanced technique than either of its constituent parts, so only embark on this when completely satisfied with soldering skills. It is the security of that first side seam that guarantees the subsequent success of this project, as there will inevitably be some annealing during the shaping process.

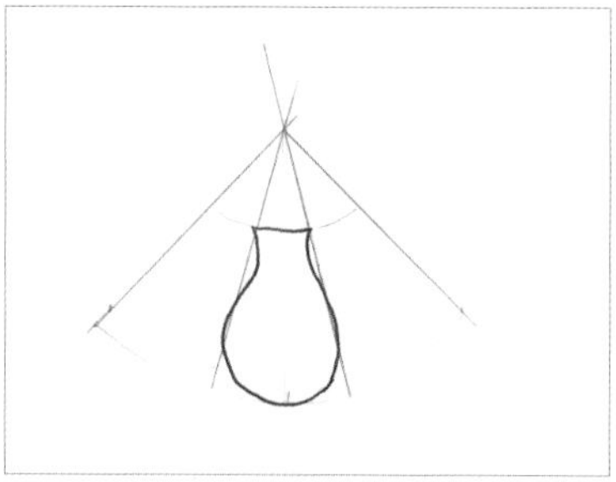

STEP 1 The pattern is made by drawing a line from just inside the widest points, top and bottom. If the object is flared these two lines on each side will meet at a central point. Draw two arcs from the top and base of the vessel. Measure the top diameter and multiply this by 3.14. Use a large compass to mark this width. If top and bottom are the same width, the blank will be a rectangle 3.14 times the diameter.

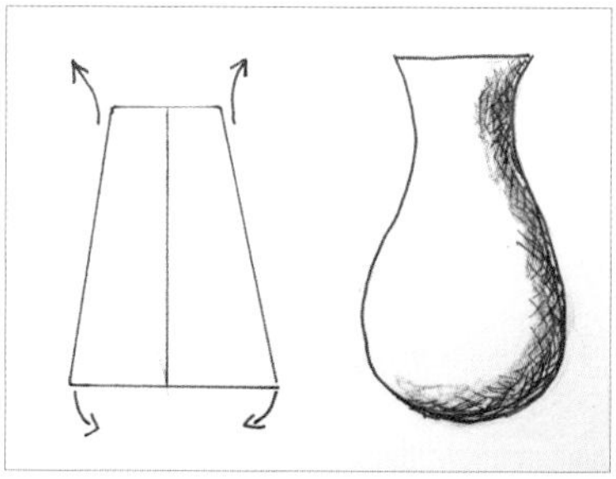

STEP 2 The starting outline, either a truncated cone or cylinder, will be shaped to fill out the body and top of the object, changing its profile from straight sided to curved. The pattern can be shorter than the proposed design because the additional raising will increase the overall height somewhat.

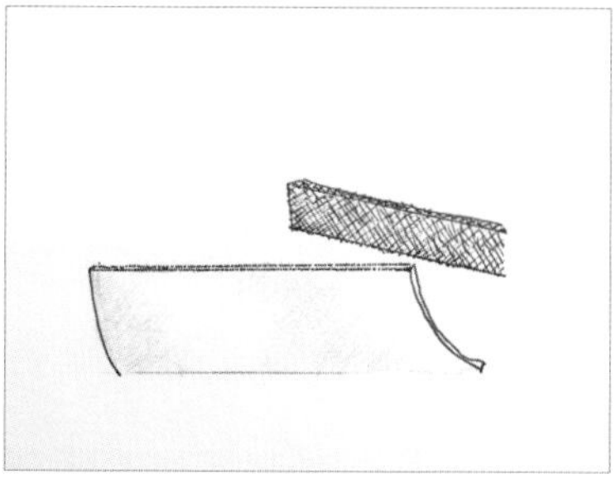

STEP 3 The blank is placed in a vice so that the edge can be filed. They are then tapped with a file corner/edge to spread and roughen them along the full length. This is like caulking.

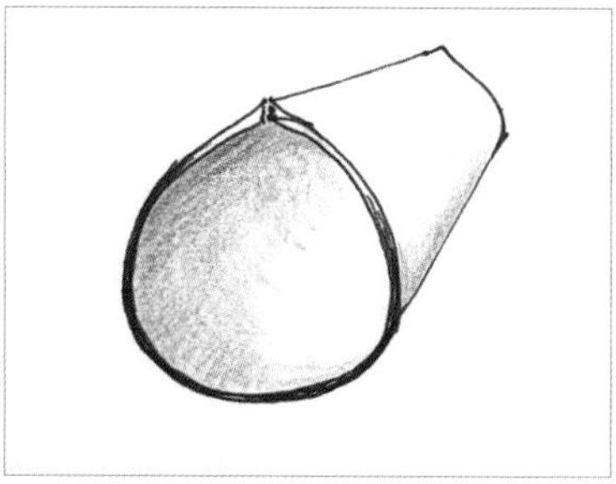

STEP 4 Press the prepared blank around a forming tool to push the edges together. In cross section this will be a fattish teardrop shape, which provides a greater contact area along the seam. Use binding wire as before to maintain contact during soldering.

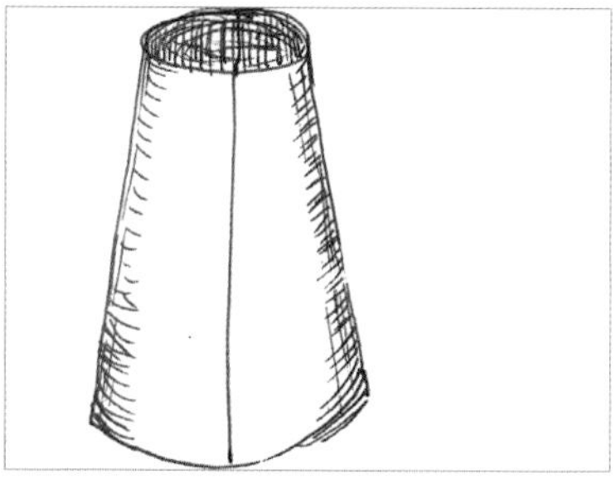

STEP 5 Solder as described earlier but use a stick of enamelling solder for this join. It will need a hotter temperature than hard solder, so watch for the rise in temperature with a snippet of solder at the end of the seam. Rest the piece for a moment before quenching, then pickle and rinse. Shape the piece on the mandrel and remove excess solder before the next step.

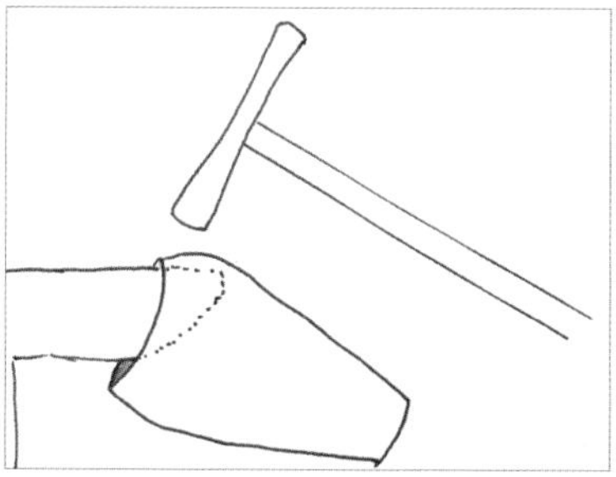

STEP 6 Work the open-ended form on a raising stake to draw the base inwards. This will develop the curved profile in the lower portion of the vessel.

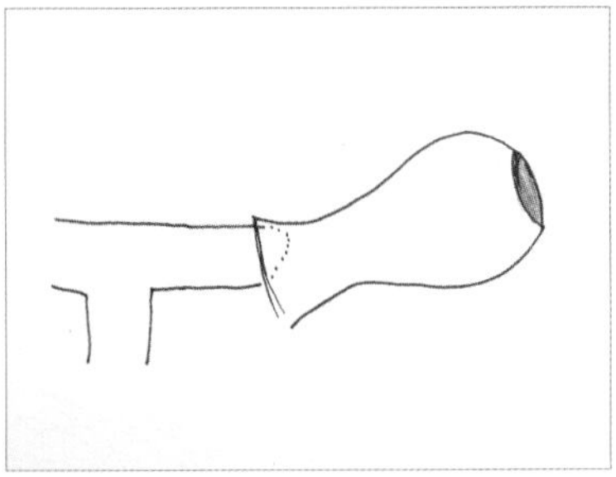

STEP 7 Shape the neck in a similar way using a raising hammer on a stake to achieve the curved profile in the upper portion of the vessel. Anneal as often as needed during the shaping stages.

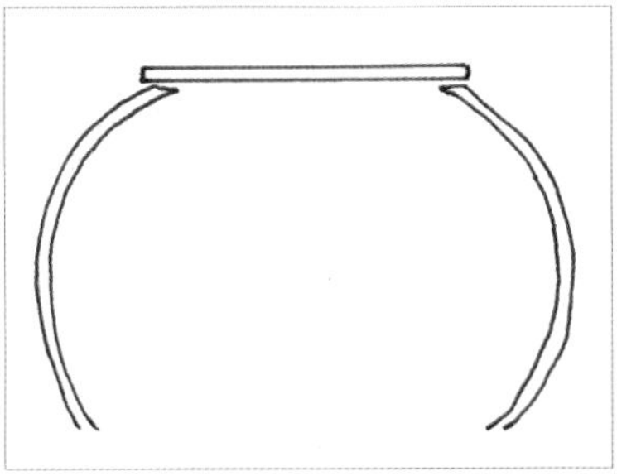

STEP 8 When the aperture at the base is sufficiently reduced, file the bottom edge through the full thickness of the wall to make a totally flat surface. Cut a base sheet from slightly thicker sheet, such as 1.2mm, and solder this on with hard solder.

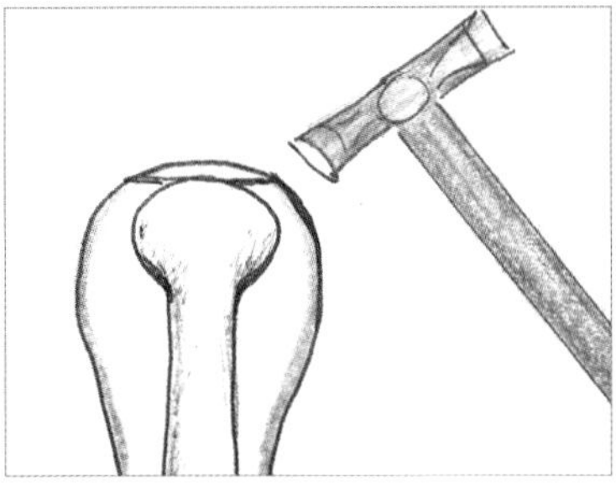

STEP 9 File off excess silver and solder before forming over a round-ended stake. The base can be formed into a smooth, continuous curve.

STEP 10 Complete the shaping and planishing over the whole surface of the piece. The vessel will stand on a base wire. Make a circular foot from chunky square wire.

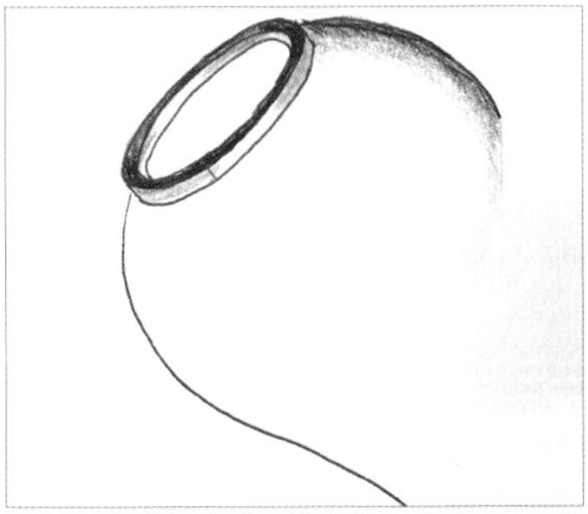

STEP 11 Join the base wire to the underside of the vessel so that it conceals the base seam. Use easy solder for this final seam.

Seamed vessels.

CHAPTER 12

Scaling Up Construction

CANDLESTICKS

A candlestick or pair of candlesticks is a chance to scale up and make something that could be somewhat larger than the previous projects. Due to the nature of a design like this, it is worth thinking about the techniques that would be best employed to create a piece that might be fairly tall. Apart from any possible height, a candlestick must be very stable and may contain several elements. Candles have to fit firmly into a holder that will keep them vertical, with the consideration that this part can be removable for cleaning and changing the candles. If the candle holder is removable, that in turn must fit securely into a specially designed part of the overall structure.

In other words, there is quite a lot of planning to include in the design process including the choice of candles. Firstly it is worth noting that most candles found on the high street or supermarket come in standard widths that will more or less fit into most commercially made candlesticks. However there are also lots of other shapes and sizes of candle out there, so start by researching whether to opt for tall or short, chunky or slender, straight or tapered. Once the type and proportion of candle has been decided, this will help determine whether the candlestick is going to stand quite high or be low and sit nearer to the table surface.

Forged candlestick.

A silver candlestick is meant to be functional, but at the same time is most definitely an ornament to adorn the table. Any design must conform to the few structural basics already mentioned such as being stable and holding the candle completely vertical, but it should also appear balanced in aesthetic terms. A candlestick should appear complete whether the candle in it is brand new or partly burnt down. Candlesticks frequently come as a pair although it is not obligatory for both to be exactly the same. Flouting conventions can provide so many more opportunities to play about with design possibilities. Beyond the single candle holder, there are those candlesticks which are designed for two candles which introduces further technical, functional and aesthetic considerations. A candelabra is usually for more than two candles, requires more of everything technically and will cost substantially more to make because of the silver needed. After looking at the general pointers such as scale, it is worth reviewing some of the techniques that have been covered in previous chapters.

Making the candlestick

Forging is an ideal candidate for structural and sculptural forms. Forged elements can be soldered together to make dramatic pieces, which are strong without having to be too heavy visually. The possible disadvantage of large forged elements is holding the work in position while parts such as a base are soldered on. With clever use of clamps or binding wire, this need not be an impediment to using a combination of constructed forged elements. Where a larger scale is being tried for the first time it is vital to test out any trial pieces in copper. What may seem viable on the sketchpad does not always translate so easily into a complex three-dimensional form.

Another approach to overcoming the technical difficulties of soldering a tall and unwieldy form is to make the piece in a totally different way. The principal structure can be created in another material entirely, such as wood, and have added adornments pinned or attached.

When designing something requiring a central 'trunk' or main upright, there will have to be some sort of appropriate tooling to use for forming any hollow vertical structure such as wooden dowel if no steel tool is available. Making a fairly tall, thin tubular structure can be quite difficult because of the problems of aligning a seam on such a tight curve; however it may be worth investigating specialist materials from bullion dealers such as larger sizes of silver tube. There is a good selection of different sizes of tubing, which can be cleverly employed in the design of a candlestick. This is a way of producing height without the weight of a solid piece of metal and allows the design to be focused on a beautiful base and complementary candle holder at the top. In this way, individual elements can be created as units which are assembled and soldered together or designed so that they can be taken apart for storage.

Other materials

A large project such as a candlestick is also an opportunity to try incorporating other materials that provide structure, strength, colour or contrast. Wood has long been used as a material with silver and resins can be cast for larger pieces of coloured material. Obviously heat from a lit candle has to be considered as a risk factor, so do not design something using a flammable material which will be anywhere near the candle flame as it burns down. Wood has the advantage in that it is inexpensive, readily available and easy to carve or shape. It can be stained or polished to emphasize a contrast with the silver.

Resin provides colour and as a liquid that is cast, it can be used like wood to create or enhance a structural element such as the base. Colour can also be introduced into a design with set stones or enamel. Vitreous enamel has a long history as an ornamental material used with silver but as it requires great skill to execute to a professional standard, many smiths use the specialist services of an enameller to undertake this part of a project. Cold enamel is an easier material to work with, as it does not need to be fired at high temperatures in a kiln but can be set in a domestic oven. Like resin or wood it cannot be used too near to the candles or candle holder, but is otherwise a good way to introduce colour to surfaces without the technical demands of vitreous enamel.

Varying the design

Below are instructions for a simple single candlestick using forged elements.

The proposed form is not very complex and relies on the piece being well enough balanced to stand on two legs with two arms to add some reflective surfaces. This piece can be made to any scale, so rather than suggest precise material requirements the project should be regarded as an introduction so that the maker can decide how big to go.

This design has one single, central candle holder but could be adapted for two with the addition of an extra pair of legs to supply greater stability.

The design of a candlestick can take on many forms, as long as it can hold a candle securely. The candle holder

Tools

- Forging, planishing and texturing hammers
- Mallet
- Steel flat plate
- Stakes to support the various curves being formed
- Drill and drill bit to match size of candle holder seat tube

Materials

- Silver rod for the arms and legs, either heavy square or rectangular section silver
- Silver sheet for the candle holder, 0.8mm thick
- Short piece of chunky tube or wire/rod for the candle holder

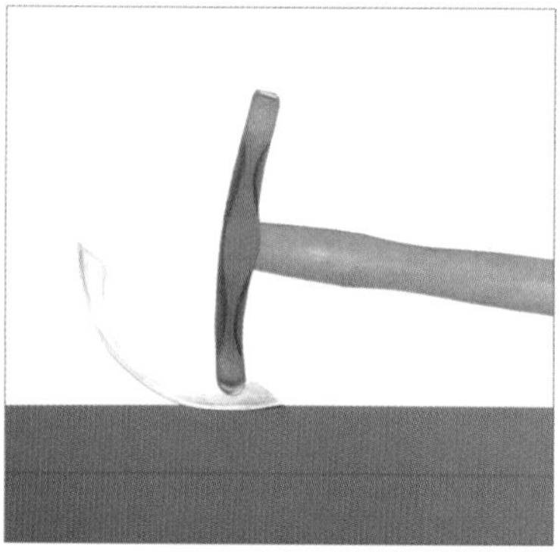

STEP 1 Prepare the design as both a drawing and a model to refine the proportions and stance of the piece. Use the model or drawing for comparison during production.

STEP 2 Spread and flatten each end of the rod and anneal when hard. Repeat until the desired shape and size are achieved for both the legs and arms. Anneal as needed.

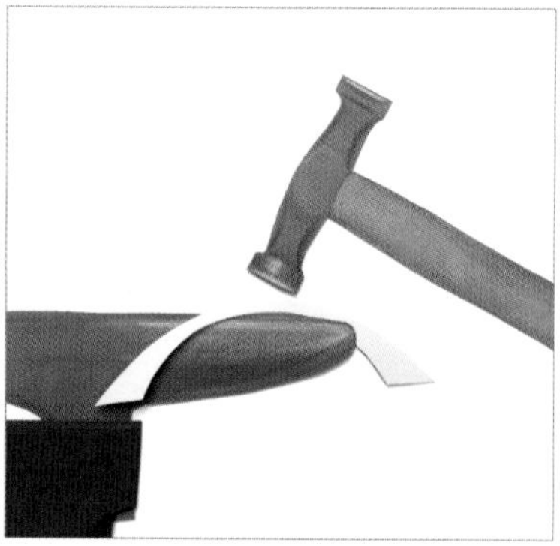

STEP 3 Planish these parts before filing and finishing. Check the shape carefully as once joined it will not be possible to alter the form.

STEP 4 The arms and legs are joined in the centre. To create a rigid structure they must be soldered together. File the contact area flat for a solid join and bind or clamp together before soldering.

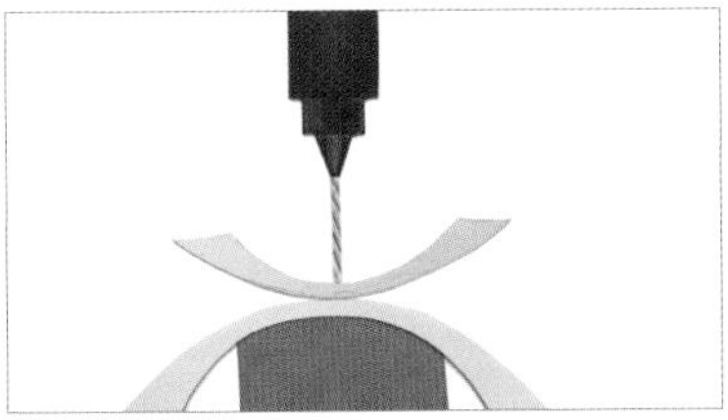

STEP 5 The candle holder will sit in the centre of this structure so carefully measure and mark the spot for the drill hole. Support the candlestick on a block of wood before drilling.

STEP 6 The candle holder. In this design the holder is in the form of a little hammered bowl with a slightly concave top with a hole for the candle. It will have a peg at the base, which locates in the drill hole made in Step 5. Start by making the cup; cut out a silver circle and form this in a doming block.

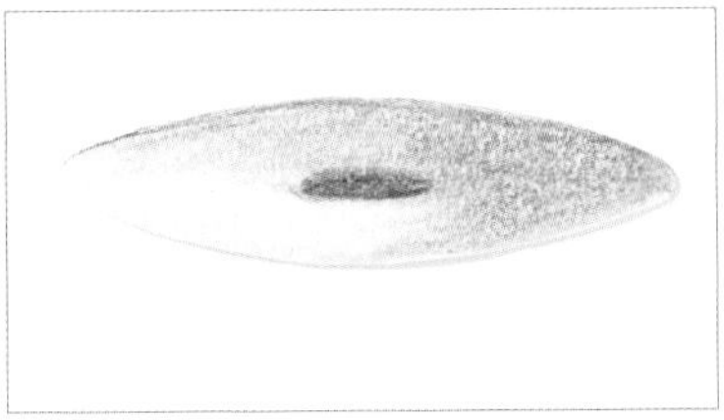

STEP 7 Cut a disc of sheet for the top of the cup. It must have a central hole for the candle and be slightly dished to create a concave form.

STEP 8 Make a sleeve for the candle to sit in; it can be slightly shorter than the depth of the cup. File the edges level.

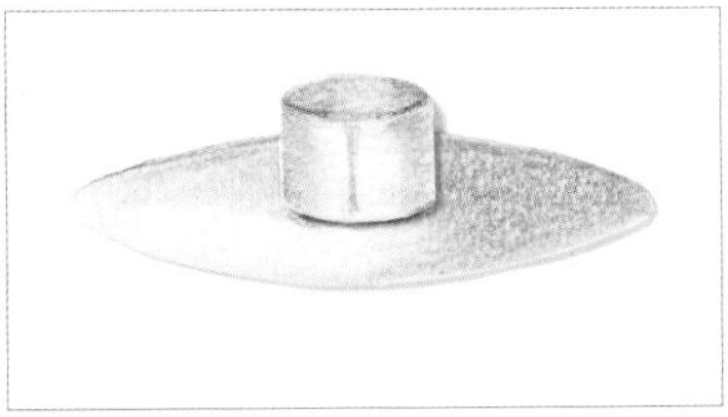

STEP 9 Solder the sleeve to the underside of the top of the candle holder. The sleeve fits over the central hole, creating a lined support for the candle. Pickle after soldering.

STEP 10 File the edge of the cup for a good fit with the underside of the top disc and solder the two parts together. The sleeve to hold the candle is now inside the cup.

STEP 11 The holder will sit in the central drill hole in the candlestick. The holder is removable but should be a firm fit. Make a peg or rod to fit this hole firmly.

STEP 12 Solder the peg to the centre of the underside of the holder so that when completed it fits securely and can hold a candle vertically without toppling or wobbling.

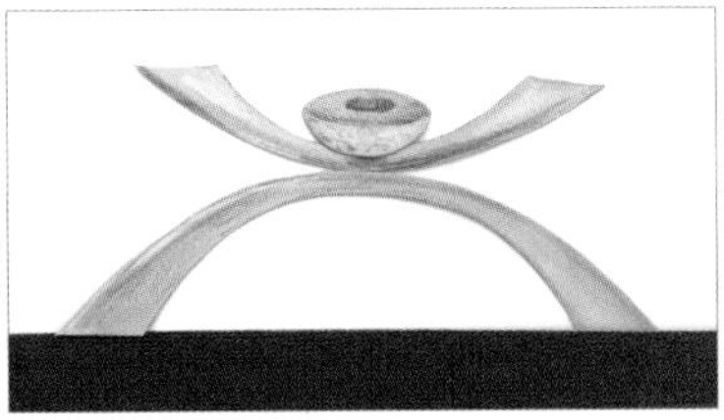

STEP 13 After completing the two elements there may need to be some minor adjusting. Check that the feet are stable and emery if necessary before finishing.

element of this project can be adapted and altered to suit all shapes and sizes of candle, or even used on its own as a method of constructing a candlestick.

CHAPTER 13

Finishing and Polishing

This has already been discussed at various points throughout the book but the finish of an object is often what it will be defined by, so with this in mind it is worth a recap. A finished object does not need to be polished if that is not its intended look. Highly polished silver can look absolutely stunning, but there is no rule that says it must be so. Many smiths will opt to have surfaces that are lightly abraded to give a softer, whiter finish to the metal; in other words it may not be shiny but it is finished. A matt or satin surface will reflect less of its surroundings but will still be light enough to look 'silver'. Oxidized silver has been deliberately tarnished to create a black surface. This works particularly well on textured silver, although some smiths have used it to totally blacken an object. As this finish can be cleaned off, it has to be sealed to protect it.

Hammered surfaces, if well executed, may need little extra work because the highly polished working face of a planishing hammer leaves the silver with a dappled polish that is a very effective way of finishing an object. Planished surfaces can seem so simple but hammer control is the key to creating this charming, twinkly surface. Just a single miss-hit can leave an unsightly chip in the silver. Fortunately it is possible to remedy such accidents by tapping carefully around the offending blemish. Make sure that the silver is in contact with the stake beneath it and always adjust the angle of the hammer so that it strikes the work squarely. Hammering at the wrong angle is usually the cause of marks on the surface.

Planishing is often the last process as a piece of silver is completed, which is why it is always stressed that the planishing hammer should be kept in top condition. Never use the planishing hammer for anything other than tapping a silver surface. The planishing itself is a surface of many tightly overlapping flat areas that give the impression of smoothness but is in fact slightly faceted on close inspection. If an object is not being left with this finish, these subtle facets must be abraded away.

POLISHING

All polishing is the action of replacing existing scratches with finer scratches. Coarse file marks are removed by working the surface with a finer file. Those finer marks are then removed with a medium grit emery paper. If doing the finishing by hand, do not move to the next grade before all the marks from the preceding one have been rubbed down. In this way the surface gradually becomes refined with finer and finer scratches, which eventually are no longer visible as marks. Having a flat piece of wood or MDF to stick emery paper onto is an efficient way to level off flat areas and making emery sticks of different grades is an easy and efficient way to work.

Use flat wood of a similar size to a large file and stick 'wet or dry' emery paper onto it with double-sided tape. It is useful to make a few sticks of different grades so they are to hand when needed. Make a note of the grade on the handle area. Odds and ends of emery paper are always useful to keep for cleaning and finishing small areas that are tricky to reach. As the emery paper gets clogged with particles, it can be rinsed in water and left to dry. If cutting the sheet of emery into smaller pieces, make a note on the back of the grade so that the right piece is always used. The grades of emery paper are worked through to a very fine grit, such as 5,000, at which point the surface is ready for a loose polishing compound.

Traditionally, most polish comes from geological deposits such as sand, grit, silica or calcium carbonate. Calcium carbonate is like chalk or talc and is sometimes referred to as 'whiting'. It is the thick sludge found in most popular metal polishes, for example Brasso. This is a trade name; it is perfectly safe to use on silver and has nothing specifically to do with brass. To make a similar polish, just mix up whiting powder with water or even a little oil and the effectiveness will be about the same as the ready-made products from a hardware store.

A finer polishing material is used for the last stage; this is rouge. Rouge is also from a natural material and is very finely ground ferric oxide/iron oxide. The particles are smaller than the whiting-based polishes, so rouge is used for the final finish of an object and it will create a really high shine. It is sold as a powder in loose form that can be mixed with water or other medium and buffed over the surface of metal. For hand polishing, use Brasso and rouge with cotton wool and buff off with a soft polishing cloth or even suede. Hand finishing is obviously slower than by motor, but it does not take too long where small projects are concerned and using emery sticks is an efficient method to get to the polishing stage.

Motorized polishers

For those with the space for a polishing motor, this does all of the above mechanically. A motorized wheel spins round and the work is held against it, polishing the surface. Most hobby grinding tools are not quite powerful enough to customize into a polishing motor. They should be able to withstand pressure while spinning so should have a robust motor of ½ to 1 horsepower. Look for a polisher that has two spindles so that there can be a different mop on each side. There must be efficient dust extraction – an open window does not count. The dust must be drawn away via an inbuilt extractor or something made from a vacuum cleaner that collects the fine particles of lint that come from the mops while they spin at speed. There should also be a housing constructed around the back of the motor and spindles. When working at the polishing motor, wear either goggles or a clear visor, always with a dust mask. It can be messy, so overalls are a good idea too.

The first stage is to buff the work with a hard polishing mop and a matching polishing compound such as tripoli. Tripoli is a composite made of finely ground-up rock called rottenstone, mixed with tallow or wax. It has what is called a 'cutting' action, which means it is similar to the emery papers in that it will be more abrasive than soft buffing. There are a large number of specialist polishes with slightly different grades and properties, but in general a first polish is done with a hard mop or wheel made of felt. The final buffing to bring up a high shine is done with a soft cotton mop, sometimes called 'swansdown', with rouge as the polish. This rouge is not in powder form but like the tripoli is packed into a hard tallow-based block, which is held to the wheel as it spins round.

Once the wheel is loaded with polish, the silver is held firmly against it and kept moving so that all areas are equally polished or buffed. The work must be held at the correct angle or it can be whipped away by the speeding mop. It is essential to learn how to use this equipment in the correct manner, as it can be dangerous if not done according to best health and safety practice. Polishing at the motor is very messy so both the silver and the smith will need a good wash afterwards. Polishing by motor is a much quicker way to finish work but it is not essential for producing a well-finished object. Much of what determines the finish is what has been done during the whole process of making the piece.

Other finishes

Textured finishes, such as very fine cross pein hammer work, punched designs and decorative finishes, will not require any of the abrasives mentioned above because these surfaces have already been prepared. All that is needed is either a light buffing with a soft cloth or for a more satin finish, a medium-fine abrasive. Tools can be used to distress the surface of metal deliberately such as files, hammers, punches or small hand-held motors with burrs or other tools. Always test power tools extensively before committing to silver because anything that is too deep or gouging would be very difficult to rectify if not satisfactory. All of these textured, roughly abraded or punched and tapped surfaces may need absolutely nothing further done.

Small objects that have twisted wires or busy textures may fit inside a barrel polishing machine. This is not suitable for flat surfaces, as they will be left with tiny dents and stipples from the barrelling compound, which is steel shot of various shapes. The barrel polisher is more of a jeweller's tool but may on occasion be suitable for some items of smithing. Because the barrel shot is made up of different shapes of ball bearings, tiny torpedo shapes and smooth needles, it must only be used on patterned surfaces or twisted wire.

For a softer surface on silver, various fine abrasives such as pumice powder can be used. It is a fine, grey abrasive dust, which is the by-product of volcanic eruptions. It can be used to create a soft blurred or matt appearance on silver and is either rubbed over the surface randomly or in a specific direction. It can be applied on damp cotton wool or an old toothbrush. Pumice is also sold in block form for use as an abrasive during the finishing stages of a project. Another product that can be used for a satin finish by hand is a garyflex block. This product is a rubber block loaded with gritty particles. It is designed to be used as an abrasive but the finest grade leaves an attractive satin surface and is fairly easy to use, being in an easy-to-hold little brick.

Finishing or polishing materials other than metal can be done using all of the wet or dry emery papers mentioned above. Resin and plastics can be polished with metal polish but are better done by hand, due to the heat generated by a motor. Wood can be emeried down to the finest grades as well, but does not need to be polished as such. Instead it is best to be lightly oiled with linseed oil or rubbed over with Renaissance Wax. This seals and protects surfaces and can be used on a wide range of materials. It can also be used on oxidized silver to protect a deliberately darkened surface.

Creating a beautiful finish to a piece of work does not have to entail lots of expensive, bulky equipment – it will take a little time and dedication, but no more than making the piece in the first place. In some instances the projects will be fairly quick to complete and of course these techniques can be revisited again and again for re-interpretation as skills levels develop. The whole subject of silversmithing really is vast, but a surprising amount can be achieved by gaining confidence with the basics of manipulating metal. Learning to anticipate how it will behave when worked in a particular way will open the door to numerous further projects. Don't be afraid of experimenting in base metal and remember that confidence only comes through practice, and practice makes perfect.

Best wishes and happy hammering.

FINDING SUPPLIES

For base metal it is worth looking for local stockists or even scrap metal suppliers who will have lots of copper wire/cable or even an old water boiler. To recycle these, the insulation needs to be cut off first. It is fairly soft and easy but messy to remove. This material may not be recyclable, so should be disposed of with general waste. Once the insulation has been removed the copper boiler can be cut up. Wear sturdy work gloves when handling because cut edges can be very sharp. If possible, drill a hole large enough for a small bladed jigsaw to fit through so the whole boiler can be opened out. The full size is very unwieldy so instead opt to cut it either with a saw or shears into sheets about 300mm/roughly 1 foot square. There will probably be a fine residue on the surface of the copper, which will burn off when it is annealed and flattened ready for use.

Plastics are used by sign makers or shop fitters so local firms may often offer offcuts for free or at a reasonable rate. Look in a local business directory to find the nearest workshop and ask to have a rummage through their offcuts.

Resins and cold enamel are available through various online suppliers and from the large jewellery supplier Cooksongold. Resin is a liquid that should be stored somewhere well ventilated and not exposed to very low or high temperatures.

Silver suppliers

- Argex is based in Birmingham; visit their website for online orders at: www.argex.co.uk
- Betts Metals is based in Birmingham and their website is: www.bettsmetalsales.com
- Cooksongold has a shop in Birmingham and London or visit the website: www.cooksongold.com

Tools suppliers

The internet is awash with suppliers of tools. In general, cheap steel tools will not be finished to such a great standard but with care may be suitable. Stakes and specialist hammers are the most expensive items and there is quite a range of quality and price, so spend some time researching before deciding what and where to buy. Good quality files are worth the extra price. A few different shapes and cuts of Swiss files make for a sound investment because they will last if properly cared for. Other hand tools such as pliers are worth paying a little extra for to get the better quality, because these should be more durable. A bench drill is a less specialist tool and will be available from several suppliers, so once the size has been decided check out the price and delivery costs for the best option. Local hardware and DIY stores will have bench vices and other more general-purpose tools for measuring, such as steel rules or dividers.

Specialist suppliers

- axminster.co.uk is mainly a woodworking tool supplier but have good selection of Swiss files at a competitive price. They also sell machinery.
- bettmetalsales.com Betts metals are a specialist firm supplying bullion, tools and equipment.
- cooksongold.com Cooksons are a specialist supplier of bullion, tools and equipment.

Some suppliers use the description 'jewellery tools' as a generic description for all their tools; however, by scrolling through the lists there are sure to be stakes and hammers which are suitable for the silversmith.

GLOSSARY OF TECHNIQUES, TERMS AND TOOLS

Abrasives Natural or sometimes synthetic materials used to abrade or scratch away minute amounts of material from the surface of metal. Abrasives can wear away file marks and surface blemishes. Commonly used examples of abrasives are emery paper/wet or dry paper, pumice in powder or lump form, steel wool.

Alloy This is the term to describe any metal made up of two or more metals. Some metals are not used much in their pure form, as they are too soft. Sterling silver is a combination of 92.5 per cent pure silver and 7.5 per cent copper.

Anneal This is a process of heating the metal to restore its malleability. Annealing occurs at a non-critical temperature (before melting point) that allows the crystalline structure of the metal to become realigned enough to be readily workable. The temperature for annealing varies a little depending on the metal concerned, but at low light levels it will appear dull red. At this point it must be plunged into water to halt the process at just the right time.

Anticlastic raising A metal-forming technique to stretch metal in axes or planes creating complex curved forms.

Anvil A heavy iron block either free-standing or on a bench or tree trunk. There are both flat and curved working surfaces.

Argotect A product that inhibits oxides forming on the surface of heated silver. It is used as paste mixed with methylated spirit to keep firestain at bay. Only use in a well ventilated workshop.

Assay This is a test to prove the purity of a precious metal object. The word 'assay' comes from the French language and means to test and confirm what an object is made from. This testing started over 700 years ago and is an early example of trading standards.

Bezel This is more of a jewellery term but it refers to a collar or flat ring to encompass a feature such as a gemstone or to provide a rim to fit into another part, such as an inner sleeve on a box.

Binding wire Iron wire that is used to tie a seam or pieces of work together whilst they are being soldered.

Borax A flux used for soldering silver or copper. It is often in the form of a compressed cone that is ground in a porcelain dish with water to create a paste. Borax is also available in powder form, which can also be used as a flux.

Burnisher A polished steel hand tool about the size of a pencil, which is rubbed over the surface of metal to shine and harden a particular area.

Casting An ancient method of creating sculptural forms in solid metal. In particular, the technique of lost wax casting has a very long history. A model is made in wax, which is then encased in plaster with a pouring hole. When the plaster is heated, the wax melts away leaving a cavity ready to be filled with molten metal. Casting is a huge subject with lots of varying methods.

Caulking Tapping an edge to thicken it for aesthetic or structural effect.

Chasing This decorative technique is used to incise lines, hollows and patterns onto the front surface of metal with a steel tool, which is tapped onto the surface with a hammer. Chasing is used on its own, to create linear patterns and unbroken lines, and is often used in conjunction with repousse.

Chenier This is a French word meaning 'tube'. Both words are used interchangeably.

Cotter pins Also known as split pins. These are steel pins for holding work in place while it is being soldered.

Crucible This is a ceramic container in which precious metal scraps can be melted down for recycling into an ingot.

Dividers An adjustable two-pronged tool for marking a circle or arc on metal. Dividers are similar to a compass and can also be used for making comparative measurements.

Doming block A steel block with a series of progressively smaller hemispherical hollows for forming sheet metal into dome shapes. It is used with round-ended doming punches.

Draw bench The draw bench is a structure that holds a draw plate in position with a pulley attached to a handle. Although very useful, it is not absolutely essential as a draw plate can be mounted in a bench vice and used by hand.

Draw plate A thick steel plate with graded holes for reducing the diameter of wire. There are plates for various shapes of wire, such as round, square, rectangular, half round, triangular and so on.

Draw tongs These are the heavy-duty tongs used to pull wire through the draw plate. They can either hook onto a bench pulley or be hand held for drawing down wire.

Electro forming Like electro plating, layers of pure metal are deposited on a pattern or form made of wood, plastic or wax. The thickness of the deposit is greater than in electro plating and is deep enough for this to be a means of manufacturing an object in metal. It is used as an alternative to casting and to create complex sculptural forms.

Enamel Enamel is powdered glass that is fused onto the surface of silver, copper or gold. It can be heated by a torch or fired in a kiln for greater accuracy. Enamel is temperature sensitive and will not melt and fuse unless hot enough, but must not be overheated or it will become discoloured and appear burnt.

Engraving This is done with sharp 'v'-shaped tool called a graver. A small channel is scraped out of the surface to create ornamental details, carved textures or lettering. Hand engraving is a skill similar to drawing on metal, but much harder to do beautifully.

Etching An acid or other corrosive material is used to dissolve away exposed areas of metal to create patterns and textures. A solution of nitric acid is the most common for etching silver, although other substances can be used.

File Files are made of steel and are covered with teeth that will remove metal when pushed away across the surface. The teeth are arranged in one direction so the file only works efficiently when drawn across the metal in a forward motion. Needle files are small for working jewellery or small details; larger files are called hand files or engineer's files.

Firescale The temporary dull surface that is caused by oxidation when heating the metal. It is removed by cleaning in pickle.

Firestain A dark shadow that occurs on or just below the surface of sterling silver after heating. It becomes more evident with repeated or prolonged heating and is caused by copper in the sterling alloy mixing with oxygen. This is often only visible after polishing and is removed by abrasives.

Flux A medium used to protect surfaces from oxidation during soldering. The action of the heat and air accelerates the tarnishing/oxidation of the metal and this inhibits the solder from bonding to the seam surfaces. Borax, Auflux, Tenacity and Easyflo are all trade-named fluxes.

Fly press The fly press was the work horse of the Industrial Revolution. It needs quite a bit of space in the workshop. This machine does the same as a hydraulic press, but with greater physical effort.

Fold forming This is a technique for forging and hammer forming folded sheet metal. It was developed in the late twentieth century by the Canadian silversmith Charles Lewton-Brain.

Forging Changing the shape/section/profile/length of rod or wire through hammering.

Hallmark Hallmarking is an ancient method of marking metal to show that it has been assayed and is of a known purity such as sterling or Britannia silver. Traditional hallmarks include the maker's initials, a symbol to describe the purity, a symbol to show where it was assayed and a letter of the alphabet for the year.

Hydraulic press This is a machine that uses hydraulic pressure to press out flat sheet into three-dimensional forms.

Ingot This is made by pouring molten metal into an ingot mould. Some smiths will recycle their own scrap into an ingot, which must then be hammered and rolled flat for sheet or formed into wire. Metal can be stored in ingots – this technique of recycling and storage is as old as the history of metalworking.

Linishers This is a power tool not unlike a sanding belt, but for speedy filing or abrading of a surface. As with all power tools, extreme caution must be used not to remove too much metal due to its speed and efficiency. It is not an essential tool as careful filing is often an efficient way to neaten and refine work.

Malleability Metal that has been annealed is malleable. This property describes soft, flexible metal, which does not have any spring in it and can be easily formed.

Mallet A rawhide, wood, horn or nylon/synthetic hammer that is used for shaping metal without marking the surface. Some mallets are weighted so they have the power to form metal with a diffuse blow but leave no dents or blemishes on the surface being worked.

Mandrel This is a long, tapered rod of steel for shaping circle forms as well as bangles and rings.

Metal fatigue Overworking a piece of metal will cause it to become brittle and it can crack. Metal fatigue refers to the point where metal has become damaged from repeated compression or distortion. To avoid this happening, work must be annealed frequently during the making process.

Metallurgy The scientific study of metals and their properties. It is not necessary to have extensive knowledge of metallurgy but it is very useful to understand why metal behaves as it does and how to use it optimally.

Micrometer A device for accurately measuring the thickness or gauge of a piece of metal. This is a handy tool to have in the workshop. Unknown sizes of wire and sheet or offcuts can be measured to determine their usefulness for a given project.

Mokume Gane This is a Japanese technique for creating metal made from many layers of differently coloured alloys. A few layers including silver are joined together, then rolled before being cut or folded and joined again. In this way a multi-layered piece of metal is created which when distorted and filed exposes the different coloured metals. Due to the base metal content mokume gane cannot be hallmarked, but as it takes much skill to produce it is also highly valued.

Mordant This is the name given to etching solutions in general and comes from the French word for 'bite', describing the action of etching as the acid nibbles away at the exposed metal.

Nitric acid This acid is used in dilute form as an etching mordant.

Oxidation Oxides form naturally on the surface of silver over time; this is generally known as tarnish but oxidation is also deliberately used as a decorative contrast to polished silver.

Patina The deliberate discolouration or apparent ageing of a surface to create a contrast to brightly polished silver. Patination may not last if an object is handled regularly and it should be sealed to protect it from wearing away.

Pendant motor A motor with a flexible drive shaft that is hand held for polishing or grinding small and intricate items. This is more of a jewellery tool, though may have uses for small silversmithing components.

Pickle The generic name for the cleaning acid used to remove oxide, borax residue or firescale from recently heated work. In general pickle is dilute sulphuric acid, but citric acid can be used.

Piercing Cutting out metal with a small piercing saw. Piercing is used to cut out sheet metal for use and can be employed as a decorative technique as well. The blades are small and appear fragile, but the small size allows intricate shapes to be cut out with accuracy.

Pitch A tar-like substance that is made up of bitumen, resin and tallow. It is used to support an object while it is being formed by the decorative techniques of chasing or repousse. Pitch is often kept in a pitch bowl, a cast-iron hemisphere that can be tilted in any direction for ease of working.

Planishing A hammering technique to flatten and remove previous hammer marks. The term is derived from the French for flatten or make plain/smooth. Planishing is done with a dedicated planishing hammer, which should be kept well polished so that no blemishes are imparted onto the metal being worked.

Plating An electro chemical technique for depositing a very fine layer of metal onto the surface of an object. Gold plating is often used on the inside of silver drinking vessels. There is no gastronomic reason for this but it is a popular aesthetic choice as a finishing touch to a cup or goblet.

Polish Any substance finer than abrasives that imparts a shine to the surface of metal. Polish, like abrasives, is usually derived from a natural source, for example geological deposits such as chalk, talc or oxides. Polishing compounds are usually pressed into a waxy bar to use on a motor-driven polishing mop that buffs the metal to a high shine.

Potassium polysulphide Also known as 'Liver of Sulphur', this smelly substance is used to deliberately blacken the surface of silver. Exposure to this sulphurous substance has the effect of instantly tarnishing the metal. It is often sold as a ready-mixed compound under a trade name, for example Platinol.

Propane A gas commonly used for heating metal. It is sold in orange gas bottles and can be used as it is or with added oxygen.

Pumice A volcanic residue used in either lump form or as a powder, like very fine sand. It is used during production as a fine abrasive and also to finish matt surfaces. As it is rather dusty, it is easiest if used when wet and loaded onto a wad of cotton wool to rub over a surface.

Quench After heating, work is almost always dunked into cold water. This is called quenching. The sizzling sound of hot work spitting as it hits the cool water is one of the most evocative workshop sounds.

Raising This technique is used to hammer flat sheet into a hollow vessel form without any seams. The sheet metal is worked on a stake from the outside. It is done in stages as the sides are gradually drawn up and the top diameter/rim is reduced but never thinned.

Raising hammer A specially shaped hammer made for raising, which can of course be used for other techniques too.

Renaissance Wax This is a trade-named product that is used to seal the treated surface of patinated/oxidized silver. It can also be used to protect and seal other surfaces such as fine wood like ebony or rosewood.

Repousse A decorative technique for creating a design in relief on sheet metal. From the French verb for push, the object is worked from the back with shaped tools that push the metal out whilst it is supported in pitch. Repousse is usually used in conjunction with chasing where the work is formed from the front.

Rivet A technique for cold joining. This can be used with two or more sheets of metal or other materials that cannot be soldered. A short pin or rivet is pushed into a close-fitting hole and the ends are hammered to flatten and spread them, so that the layers are tightly held together.

Rolling mill This is a machine with two rollers that can reduce the thickness of sheet metal. The rolling mill can also be used to impress decorative textures onto the surface of sheet silver. This is called 'roller printing'. Rolling mills may also have grooved rollers for extruding square or half-round wire.

Rouge A polishing compound used to finish a surface after all other work is completed. Rouge gets its name and rusty colour from the finely ground iron oxide which is its main component. It can be used in powder form mixed with liquid for hand polishing or in a solid bar with tallow for use with a polishing mop. Rouge and water paste is also used as an inhibitor of solder.

Sandbag A disc or cushion-shaped pouch made from heavy-duty leather and filled with sand. The sandbag is used to support work while it is being formed.

Scoring Carving or scratching a deep 'v'-shaped groove into sheet metal so that it can be folded or formed with a crisp edge. A scored fold will have to be soldered after shaping, as the remaining thickness at the outside of the corner is minimal.

Scriber Known as a scribe or scriber, this is a tool for scratching a fine working line into metal when taking measurements or marking a cutting line.

Sinking A technique used to create shallow bowl forms by hammering from the inside surface of sheet metal whilst being in contact with a steel flat plate.

Soldering Joining metal together with an alloy that melts at a lower temperature than the parts being reconnected. Enamelling, hard, medium and easy are the terms used to describe solders with progressively lower melting points, which allows several joints to be soldered without damaging existing seams.

Stake A steel forming tool that is usually held in a bench vice or fixed in a tree trunk. It is used to create and support three-dimensional hollow forms.

Sulphuric acid A colourless acid that is diluted about one part acid to twelve parts water for use as a cleaning pickle for precious metal. **NB.** Never allow steel or iron to touch the acid, as this will cause a chemical change that will copper-plate any silver being cleaned.

Swage block A steel block with 'u' shaped grooves into which flat metal is pressed or hammered with a forming tool to create longitudinal hollows.

Torch A gas appliance for heating metal at a hearth for annealing or soldering.

Tweezers Brass or non-ferrous tweezers are used for taking work in and out of acid. Reverse-action steel tweezers are used for holding work during heating or picking up hot work to quench.

Vernier gauge This is a tool for precise measuring of inside or outside dimensions. An internal measurement such as the inside of a bowl or size of an aperture, or an external dimension such as the thickness of sheet or size of an object.

Work hardening When metal has been hammered, drawn, rolled, twisted or manipulated it builds up resistance and is no longer malleable. At this stage it is necessary to anneal the piece if further forming is to be done. It is generally desirable for a completed piece to be in a work-hardened state as this is less likely to dent or deform.

INDEX